EMPOWERING COMMUNITIES

A Comprehensive Guide to Rural Electrification.

By

Chukwujekwu John Okafor

Oko Obasi

ISBN: 9798854279703

Imprint: Independently published

Printed in the United States of America.

Book design by Oko Obasi

Cover design by Oko Obasi

TABLE OFCONTENTS

systems
B. Distribution network planning and grid extension strategies
C. Off-grid solutions: Mini-grids and standalone systems
D. Integration of renewable energy sources
E. Energy storage solutions for rural electrification
F. Safety standards and regulations in rural electrification

V. Operation, Maintenance, and Sustainability
A. Establishing efficient operation and maintenance protocols
B. Training local technicians and community members
C. Ensuring reliable electricity supply and troubleshooting
D. Tariff models and revenue collection strategies
E. Evaluating and optimizing system performance
F. Sustainability and long-term viability of rural electrification projects

VI. Socio-Economic and Community Development
A. Socio-economic benefits of rural electrification
B. Electrification and entrepreneurship in rural areas
C. Enhancing education and healthcare services
D. Improving quality of life and livelihood opportunities
E. Women empowerment and gender-inclusive

approaches
F. Environmental sustainability and clean energy adoption

VII. Policy, Regulation, and Institutional Framework
A. National and regional policies for rural electrification
B. Regulatory frameworks and legal considerations
C. Institutional capacity building and governance structures
D. Public-private partnerships and stakeholder collaboration
E. Financing mechanisms and incentives for rural electrification

VIII. Case Studies and Best Practices
A. In-depth analysis of successful rural electrification projects
B. Innovative approaches and technological advancements
C. Replication and scalability of successful models

IX. Future Trends and Challenges
A. Emerging technologies and their potential in rural electrification
B. Climate change and resilient electrification solutions
C. Addressing energy poverty and access gaps
D. Policy recommendations for accelerating rural electrification

X. Conclusion
A. Call to action for sustainable rural electrification
B. Encouragement for further research and collaboration.

References
About the Authors

Dedication

This book is dedicated to all the rural dwellers who desire for empowerment through rural electrification.
To our unwavering support system—our family members—who have believed in us even when we doubted ourselves.

Engr Chukwujekwu John Okafor
Oko Obasi

Chukwujekwu John Okafor and Oko
Obasi

Acknowledgements

We would like to express our immense gratitude to all the individuals who have contributed to the creation and publication of this book.

First and foremost, we extend our deepest appreciation to our families. Their love, patience, and understanding throughout this journey have been the foundation of our strength. They have been our constant source of inspiration, and we are truly fortunate to have their unwavering belief in us.

To our friends and colleagues, especially Engr Victor Meju, the Chairman of Engineering Regulation Monitoring, Anambra State Technical Committee, we are grateful for your unwavering belief in us. Your encouragement and support throughout this endeavor have been truly uplifting.

We are indebted to the numerous experts and researchers who have dedicated their time and effort to advancing the knowledge in this field. Their pioneering work has paved the way for our own exploration, and we are grateful for the wealth of information and insights they have shared.

Last but certainly not least, we extend our sincere appreciation to the readers of this book. Your interest and engagement in the subject matter have fueled our passion for writing. We hope that this book provides you with new perspectives, knowledge, and inspiration.

In conclusion, we are humbled and honored to have had the opportunity to write this book. The support and contributions of each individual mentioned above have played a pivotal role in its creation. Thank you all for being a part of this incredible journey.
With deepest gratitude,

Chukwujekwu John Okafor

Chukwujekwu John Okafor and Oko
Obasi

Obasi Oko Igbokwe

Chukwujekwu John Okafor and Oko Obasi

Preface

Welcome to "Empowering Communities: A Comprehensive Guide to Rural Electrification." This guide aims to shed light on the transformative power of rural electrification and provide valuable insights for those seeking to embark on this important journey. The electrification of rural areas has the potential to uplift communities, enhance livelihoods, and foster sustainable development.

Access to electricity is often taken for granted in urban areas, but it remains a luxury for many rural communities around the world. Lack of electricity hampers progress in various aspects of life, including education, healthcare, agriculture, and economic opportunities. It creates barriers that limit the potential and aspirations of individuals and communities, perpetuating a cycle of poverty and inequality.

However, the path to comprehensive rural electrification is not without its challenges. It requires a deep understanding of local needs, careful planning, and coordination among stakeholders. It demands innovative solutions and the utilization of appropriate technologies. It necessitates sustainable financing models and community participation. This guide aims to navigate through these challenges and present a roadmap to success.

In this comprehensive guide, we have meticulously compiled information, strategies, and best practices from experts and practitioners in the field of rural electrification. Each chapter delves into a specific aspect of the electrification process, providing practical insights, case studies, and key considerations for implementation. Whether you are a policymaker, a development organization, an entrepreneur, or a community leader, this guide will equip you with the knowledge and tools to make informed decisions and drive change.

We believe that rural electrification is not just about providing access to electricity; it is about empowering communities. It is about giving individuals the opportunity to pursue their dreams, improving their quality of life, and contributing to the development of their societies. It is about bridging the gap between urban and rural areas, ensuring that no one is left behind in the pursuit of progress.

As we embark on this journey together, let us be reminded of the profound impact that rural electrification can have on individuals, families, and entire communities. Let us recognize the immense potential that lies within these often overlooked regions. Let us join forces to create a brighter and more sustainable future for rural areas worldwide.

We hope that this guide will inspire and empower you to take action, to advocate for change, and to contribute to the electrification of rural communities. Together, we can transform lives, break barriers, and build a world where every individual has access to the transformative power of electricity.

Open these pages, absorb the knowledge within, and let us embark on this empowering journey of rural electrification.

CHAPTER 1

INTRODUCTION

"Empowering Communities: A Comprehensive Guide to Rural Electrification" is an informative and practical book that delves into the challenges, strategies, and benefits associated with providing electricity to rural areas. Authored by experts in the field, this book serves as a comprehensive resource for individuals, organizations, and policymakers seeking to understand and implement rural electrification projects. The book begins by highlighting the critical importance of access to electricity in rural communities.

Once upon a time in Awka, a bustling city in Anambra State, Nigeria, a group of determined individuals embarked on a mission to empower their community through rural electrification. Led by Chinedu, a passionate young engineer, they believed that access to electricity would transform the lives of the people in Awka.

Chinedu had grown up witnessing the challenges his community faced due to the lack of electricity.

He knew that with electricity, children could study at night, businesses could thrive, and healthcare facilities could provide better services. Determined to make a difference, Chinedu gathered a team of like-minded individuals who shared his vision.

The team worked tirelessly, engaging with community members, conducting surveys, and understanding the specific needs and aspirations of the people in Awka. They realized that the existing power infrastructure was inadequate and unreliable, leaving many areas in darkness.

Undeterred, the team explored alternative energy solutions. They discovered the potential of solar power and decided to harness the abundant sunlight in Awka to bring electricity to their community. With the support of local authorities and community leaders, they secured a plot of land to set up a solar power plant.

Months of hard work and collaboration followed. The team tirelessly installed solar panels, set up batteries for energy storage, and connected the power plant to the local distribution grid. It was a challenging endeavor, but their determination fueled their efforts.

One sunny day, as the final touches were being made, the team organized a grand unveiling ceremony. The entire community of Awka gathered, buzzing with anticipation and excitement. The atmosphere was electrifying as Chinedu, with a beaming smile, switched on the solar power plant.

As the sun's rays were converted into electricity, the streets of Awka were bathed in light. The crowd erupted in cheers and applause, overjoyed to witness the transformation taking place before their eyes. Children laughed and danced, adults embraced each other, and the sound of celebration filled the air.

The impact of electrification quickly became evident. Street vendors extended their business hours, offering their goods under the bright lights. Students gathered in communal study spaces, equipped with electricity to power their laptops and study late into the night. Local artisans were able to enhance their productivity, expanding their customer base.

The community of Awka flourished with newfound opportunities. Chinedu and his team continued their efforts, ensuring the sustainability of the project by providing maintenance and training programs to local technicians. They empowered the community to take ownership of their electricity infrastructure and instilled a sense of pride and responsibility.

Word of Awka's success spread to neighboring villages, inspiring them to embark on their own electrification journeys. The ripple effect of this transformative initiative extended beyond Awka, reaching communities far and wide, as they witnessed the power of unity and determination in bringing sustainable change.

Today, Awka stands as a shining example of what can be achieved through rural electrification. The once-dark city has become a beacon of hope and progress, empowering its people and fostering a brighter future for generations to come.

This book explores the profound impact that electrification can have on various aspects of community development, including education, healthcare, economic growth, and overall quality of life. By examining success stories from different regions, the book showcases the transformative power of electricity in empowering rural communities. One of the key strengths of "Empowering Communities" lies in its detailed examination of the challenges and barriers that hinder rural electrification efforts. The authors explore factors such as geographical constraints, financial limitations, technological considerations, and policy frameworks that can impact the implementation and sustainability of electrification projects. By providing insights into these obstacles, the book equips readers with a realistic understanding of the complexities involved in rural electrification.

Furthermore, the book offers a comprehensive guide to the planning, implementation, and management of rural electrification initiatives. It discusses various electrification technologies, ranging from centralized grid systems to decentralized solutions such as mini-grids and standalone solar systems. The authors delve into the technical aspects of each option, considering factors like resource availability, cost-effectiveness, scalability, and environmental impact. Additionally, they provide practical guidance on project management, stakeholder engagement, financing models, and policy considerations.

"Empowering Communities" emphasizes the importance of community participation and capacity-building throughout the electrification process. It advocates for inclusive approaches that involve local communities, empowering them to take ownership of the projects and ensuring their long-term sustainability. The book provides insights on engaging with community members, fostering entrepreneurship, and promoting energy literacy to create a holistic and participatory electrification ecosystem.

Overall, "Empowering Communities: A Comprehensive Guide to Rural Electrification" is a valuable resource for anyone involved in rural electrification projects. With its combination of theoretical frameworks, practical guidance, and case studies, the book equips readers with the knowledge and tools necessary to navigate the challenges and implement sustainable electrification solutions in rural areas, ultimately contributing to the empowerment and development of communities around the world.

This book begins by delving into the multifaceted nature of rural electrification, exploring the challenges and barriers that must be overcome, and highlighting the far-reaching socio-economic benefits that can be achieved. It emphasizes the importance of engaging local communities, understanding their unique energy needs, and tailoring electrification solutions that are contextually appropriate and sustainable.

Throughout the book, you will gain insights into the crucial aspects of rural electrification planning, including conducting feasibility studies, selecting suitable technologies, designing infrastructure, ensuring operation and maintenance, and addressing financial and regulatory considerations. Real-world case studies and exemplary projects will be presented, illustrating successful models of rural electrification and drawing valuable lessons from their implementation.

Moreover, this guide recognizes the integral role of policy, regulation, and institutional frameworks in driving effective electrification efforts. It provides guidance on creating an enabling environment that encourages public-private partnerships, facilitates financing mechanisms, and fosters collaboration among stakeholders at various levels.

The book also explores the broader dimensions of rural electrification, examining its impact on education, healthcare, gender equality, and environmental sustainability. It underscores the importance of holistic and inclusive approaches that empower local communities, especially women and marginalized groups, to actively participate in and benefit from electrification initiatives.

Ultimately, "Empowering Communities: A Comprehensive Guide to Rural Electrification" aims to equip its readers with the knowledge, tools, and inspiration needed to embark on transformative rural electrification journeys. By embracing the power of electricity and sustainable energy solutions, we can unlock the full potential of rural communities, foster inclusive development, and create a brighter future for all.

1.1 THE IMPORTANCE OF RURAL ELECTRIFICATION:

Rural electrification holds significant importance due to its wide-ranging impacts on individuals, communities, and overall societal development. Here are some key reasons why rural electrification is important:

Socio-Economic Development: Access to electricity in rural areas is a catalyst for socio-economic progress. It enables the establishment and growth of businesses, enhances agricultural productivity, and fosters entrepreneurship. With electricity, rural communities can engage in income-generating activities, create employment opportunities, and contribute to local economic development.

Improved Quality of Life: Electricity improves the overall quality of life in rural areas. It facilitates access to modern amenities and appliances, such as lighting, refrigeration, and communication devices. These advancements lead to improved healthcare services, better education opportunities, extended working hours, and enhanced safety and security.

Education and Digital Connectivity: Rural

electrification enables access to educational resources and technology, bridging the digital divide between urban and rural areas. It allows for the establishment of computer labs, e-learning platforms, and access to the internet. This empowers students, teachers, and communities to engage in digital literacy, distance learning, and online research, thereby expanding educational opportunities and knowledge sharing.

Healthcare and Public Services: Electricity plays a crucial role in healthcare delivery, enabling the operation of medical equipment, refrigeration for vaccines and medications, lighting in healthcare facilities, and the availability of clean water. It supports telemedicine initiatives, facilitates the use of medical devices, and improves emergency response capabilities, leading to better healthcare outcomes for rural populations.

Community Empowerment: Rural electrification empowers communities by providing them with a reliable and sustainable source of energy. It enables self-sufficiency, reduces dependence on traditional and often harmful energy sources (such as kerosene lamps or biomass), and fosters community-led development initiatives. Electricity access enables communities to take control of their own progress, promoting self-reliance and a sense of pride.

Environmental Sustainability: Rural electrification can promote the adoption of clean energy technologies, including renewable energy sources such as solar, wind, or hydro. By reducing reliance on fossil fuels and traditional biomass, it contributes to mitigating climate change, lowering carbon emissions, and improving environmental sustainability. It also helps preserve natural resources and ecosystems.

Social Inclusion and Gender Equality: Access to electricity empowers marginalized groups, including women and girls, by enabling economic activities, education, and improved healthcare. It reduces the burden of manual labor, enhances safety and security, and provides opportunities for women's entrepreneurship and income generation. Rural electrification can help bridge gender gaps and promote equality within communities.

Disaster Resilience: Electricity is vital for disaster preparedness, response, and recovery in rural areas. It supports early warning systems, emergency communication networks, and power supply for critical facilities such as emergency shelters, hospitals, and water pumping stations. Reliable electricity enables faster recovery and rehabilitation efforts following natural disasters.

By recognizing the importance of rural electrification and prioritizing its implementation, societies can unlock the potential of rural communities, bridge the development gap between urban and rural areas, and create more inclusive and sustainable societies.

1.2   Overview of the book's Purpose and Structure:

Purpose: "Empowering Communities: A Comprehensive Guide to Rural Electrification" is a book specifically designed to serve as a practical and informative resource for individuals, organizations, and policymakers involved in rural electrification projects. The purpose of this comprehensive guide is to empower engineers, policymakers, development practitioners, and stakeholders involved in rural electrification projects with the knowledge and tools they need to navigate the complex landscape of planning, designing, implementing, and sustaining electrification initiatives in rural areas. It serves as a roadmap, drawing from the collective experiences and best practices from around the world. The book aims to address the challenges, strategies, and benefits associated with providing electricity to rural areas, ultimately empowering communities and fostering their sustainable development.

Structure:

1.   Introduction: The book begins with an introduction that highlights the importance of rural electrification and its potential impact on community development. It sets the stage for understanding the significance of the subject matter.

2.   Importance of Rural Electrification: This section delves deeper into the profound impact that access to electricity can have on various aspects of rural communities, such as education, healthcare, economic growth, and overall quality of life. It showcases real-life success stories to demonstrate the transformative power of electrification.

3.   Challenges and Barriers: The book thoroughly examines the challenges and barriers that can impede rural electrification efforts. It explores factors such as geographical constraints, financial limitations, technological considerations, and policy frameworks that need to be addressed to ensure successful implementation and sustainability of electrification projects.

4.   Planning and Implementation: This section provides a comprehensive guide to planning and implementing rural electrification initiatives. It discusses various electrification technologies and

their suitability for different contexts, considering factors like resource availability, cost-effectiveness, scalability, and environmental impact. Practical guidance on project management, stakeholder engagement, financing models, and policy considerations are also included.

5. Community Participation and Capacity-Building: Recognizing the importance of community involvement, this section emphasizes inclusive approaches to rural electrification. It explores strategies for engaging with local communities, fostering entrepreneurship, and promoting energy literacy. The aim is to empower communities to take ownership of electrification projects and ensure their long-term sustainability.

6. Case Studies and Best Practices: This segment features real-world case studies and best practices from various regions and contexts. It provides valuable insights into successful rural electrification projects, highlighting key factors that contributed to their effectiveness. Readers can gain inspiration and learn from these examples.

7. Conclusion: The book concludes by summarizing the main points and reiterating the significance of rural electrification in empowering communities. It encourages readers to take action and apply the knowledge and strategies discussed throughout the book.

Overall, "Empowering Communities: A Comprehensive Guide to Rural Electrification" follows a logical and structured approach. It provides a comprehensive overview of the subject matter, offers practical guidance, and incorporates real-world examples to inspire and inform readers involved in rural electrification projects. The book equips them with the necessary knowledge and tools to overcome challenges and implement sustainable electrification solutions, ultimately contributing to the empowerment and development of rural communities.

Chukwujekwu John Okafor and Oko Obasi

CHAPTER 2

UNDERSTANDING RURAL ELECTRIFICATION

2.1   Understanding Rural Electrification: Rural electrification involves the extension of the power grid or the implementation of decentralized power systems, such as renewable energy sources, to provide electricity to these areas.

The importance of rural electrification lies in its potential to improve the quality of life for people living in rural areas. Here are some key points to understand about rural electrification:

Access to modern energy services: Rural electrification allows households, businesses, and public institutions in rural areas to have access to modern energy services. This includes lighting, cooking, refrigeration, communication, and powering appliances and equipment. Electricity can enhance productivity, enable economic activities, and improve overall living conditions.

Power grid extension: In some cases, rural electrification involves extending the existing power grid infrastructure to reach remote areas. This requires the installation of power transmission and distribution lines, transformers, and other necessary infrastructure. Grid extension can be costly and challenging due to geographical constraints, long distances, and sparse population density in rural areas.

Decentralized renewable energy solutions: In situations where grid extension is not feasible or cost-effective, decentralized solutions based on renewable energy sources like solar, wind, hydro, or biomass can be implemented. These solutions involve setting up small-scale power generation systems that cater to the energy needs of specific communities or individual households. Decentralized systems can provide reliable and sustainable electricity, reduce dependence on fossil

Chukwujekwu John Okafor and Oko Obasi

fuels, and mitigate environmental impacts.

Socio-economic benefits: Rural electrification can have wide-ranging socio-economic benefits. It improves healthcare services by enabling the operation of medical equipment, refrigeration of vaccines and medicines, and providing lighting in healthcare facilities. It facilitates education by powering schools, enabling access to computers and digital resources, and extending study hours. Electrification also promotes entrepreneurship and income-generating activities by powering small businesses and agricultural machinery, thus fostering economic growth in rural areas.

Challenges and solutions: Rural electrification faces various challenges, including high upfront costs, limited financial resources, technical constraints, inadequate infrastructure, and policy and regulatory barriers. However, innovative financing mechanisms, public-private partnerships, supportive policies, and technological advancements have been instrumental in overcoming these challenges. Additionally, community participation and capacity building are crucial for the successful implementation and sustainability of rural electrification projects.

Sustainable development goals: Rural electrification

aligns with several United Nations Sustainable Development Goals (SDGs), including SDG 7 (Affordable and Clean Energy), SDG 1 (No Poverty), SDG 3 (Good Health and Well-being), SDG 4 (Quality Education), and SDG 8 (Decent Work and Economic Growth). It contributes to poverty reduction, improved health outcomes, better education, gender equality, and environmental sustainability.

Rural electrification is a critical aspect of bridging the energy access gap and promoting inclusive development. It plays a vital role in empowering rural communities, unlocking their potential, and enabling them to participate in the broader socio-economic progress.

2.2   Definition and scope of rural electrification

Rural electrification refers to the process of providing electricity to rural and remote areas that lack access to modern energy services. It involves the extension of the electrical power grid or the implementation of decentralized power systems to bring electricity to these areas. The scope of rural electrification encompasses various aspects:

Access to electricity: The primary objective of rural electrification is to ensure that households, businesses, and public institutions in rural areas have access to reliable and affordable electricity. This includes providing electricity for lighting, cooking, refrigeration, communication, and powering appliances and equipment.

Infrastructure development: Rural electrification requires the development of electricity infrastructure in remote areas. This may involve extending the existing power grid infrastructure by installing power transmission and distribution lines, transformers, substations, and other necessary equipment. In cases where grid extension is not feasible, decentralized solutions based on renewable energy sources, such as solar, wind, hydro, or biomass, can be implemented.

Financial and economic considerations: Rural electrification projects involve financial considerations to fund the infrastructure development and operational costs. It requires investment in capital equipment, maintenance, and operation of the power systems. Additionally, economic viability assessments are important to ensure that the costs associated with providing electricity are reasonable and sustainable in the long term.

Policy and regulatory framework: The scope of rural electrification includes the formulation of policies and regulations to support and guide the implementation of electrification projects. Governments and regulatory bodies play a crucial role in creating an enabling environment by setting targets, establishing incentives, developing supportive regulations, and promoting public-private partnerships.

Socio-economic impact: Rural electrification has a significant socio-economic impact on rural communities. Access to electricity improves living conditions, enhances productivity, enables income-generating activities, promotes entrepreneurship, supports education and healthcare services, and contributes to overall socio-economic development in rural areas. It also helps bridge the digital divide by providing power for digital technologies and connectivity.

Sustainability and environmental considerations: The scope of rural electrification extends to incorporating sustainable and environmentally friendly practices. This includes promoting the use of renewable energy sources, energy efficiency measures, and reducing reliance on fossil fuels. Sustainable electrification ensures long-term energy security, mitigates climate change impacts, and minimizes adverse environmental effects.

The scope of rural electrification is multi-dimensional, encompassing technical, financial, policy, social, and environmental aspects. It aims to provide reliable and affordable electricity to rural areas, fostering inclusive and sustainable development while improving the quality of life for rural communities.

2.3   Challenges and barriers in rural electrification

Rural electrification, the process of providing access to electricity in rural areas, faces several challenges and barriers that can vary depending on the region and specific context. Here are some common challenges and barriers associated with rural electrification:

Infrastructure: Building and maintaining electricity infrastructure in rural areas can be challenging due to the lack of existing transmission and distribution networks. The remote and scattered nature of rural communities often requires extensive investments in infrastructure, including power generation, transmission lines, and distribution networks.

Affordability: Many rural communities, particularly in developing countries, face financial constraints and may not have the means to pay for electricity connections or monthly bills. The high upfront costs associated with infrastructure development and connection fees can be prohibitive for low-income households and communities.

Operational Costs: Providing electricity to rural areas with low population densities can result in higher operational costs. The costs of electricity generation, transmission losses, and maintenance of infrastructure can be comparatively higher per customer in rural areas, making it economically challenging to provide affordable and sustainable electricity services.

Financing and Investment: Securing financing for rural electrification projects can be difficult due to the perceived risks associated with serving remote and economically disadvantaged areas. Lack of access to affordable loans, investment capital, or grants can hinder the implementation of electrification projects.

Technical Challenges: Rural areas may lack skilled technicians and engineers to install, operate, and maintain electrical systems. Training and capacity-building programs are essential to address technical challenges and ensure the sustainability of electrification efforts.

Institutional Framework: The absence of a well-defined regulatory framework and institutional support can impede progress in rural electrification. Clear policies, regulations, and governance structures are necessary to attract investments, establish public-private partnerships, and coordinate the efforts of various stakeholders involved in electrification projects.

Environmental Considerations: In some cases, the location of rural communities may present environmental challenges for electrification projects. Remote areas with limited access may require environmentally friendly solutions, such as off-grid renewable energy sources, to minimize the environmental impact and ensure sustainability.

Social and Cultural Factors: Socio-cultural factors, including community acceptance, awareness, and preferences, can influence the success of rural electrification initiatives. Engaging local communities, understanding their specific needs and priorities, and involving them in decision-making processes are crucial for long-term sustainability and adoption.

Overcoming these challenges requires a multi-faceted approach that involves coordination among governments, international organizations, private sector entities, and local communities. Strategies such as innovative financing mechanisms, technology adaptation, capacity building, and policy reforms can help address these barriers and promote successful rural electrification.

2.4   Socio-economic impact of electrification in rural areas

Electrification in rural areas can have significant socio-economic impacts, bringing about positive changes in various aspects of life. Here are some key socio-economic benefits of electrification in rural areas:

Improved Living Standards: Electrification enables access to modern amenities such as lighting, refrigeration, and heating, which enhance the quality of life in rural communities. It helps eliminate the reliance on traditional, inefficient, and often hazardous energy sources like kerosene lamps and wood-burning stoves.

Education and Knowledge: Access to electricity facilitates educational opportunities in rural areas. Schools can have adequate lighting and use electronic devices like computers and projectors, enabling better teaching and learning experiences. Students can access educational resources through digital platforms, broadening their knowledge base and improving academic outcomes.

Economic Productivity and Job Creation: Electrification drives economic growth and productivity in rural areas. It enables the establishment of small businesses, such as welding shops, tailoring units, and food processing ventures, which rely on electricity for their operations. Access to electricity also attracts investments and industries to rural areas, creating employment opportunities and boosting local economies.

Agricultural Development: Rural electrification supports agricultural activities by providing power for irrigation systems, machinery, and processing facilities. Electric pumps and motors can improve water management and increase crop yields. Post-harvest processing and storage facilities, powered by electricity, help reduce food wastage and add value to agricultural produce.

Healthcare and Public Services: Electricity is vital for healthcare services in rural areas. It enables the functioning of medical equipment, refrigeration for vaccines and medicines, and lighting for clinics and hospitals. Access to electricity also facilitates communication systems, enabling better coordination of emergency services and access to information.

Enhanced Connectivity and Communication: Electrification brings about improved connectivity and communication infrastructure in rural areas. It enables the installation of telecommunication towers, providing access to mobile networks and internet connectivity. This connectivity allows rural communities to access information, participate in e-commerce, and connect with the broader world, opening up opportunities for social and economic advancement.

Social Empowerment and Gender Equality: Electrification can have a positive impact on gender equality and social empowerment in rural areas. It reduces the burden on women and children who traditionally spend significant time on household chores like collecting firewood and water, by introducing modern energy-efficient solutions. Access to electricity also fosters entrepreneurship among women, enabling them to start their businesses and generate income.

It is worth noting that the successful implementation of rural electrification programs requires a holistic approach, considering factors like affordability, infrastructure development, capacity building, and sustainable energy solutions. Additionally, community participation and the involvement of local stakeholders are crucial for long-term sustainability and maximizing the socio-economic benefits of electrification in rural areas.

2.5 Case studies showcasing successful rural electrification projects:

Here are a few examples of successful rural electrification projects from different parts of the world:

Bangladesh's Rural Electrification Program: Bangladesh has made remarkable progress in rural electrification through its Rural Electrification Program (REP). The program, initiated in 1978, aimed to provide electricity access to remote and underserved areas. By adopting a cooperative model, the program established numerous rural electric cooperatives, known as Palli Bidyut Samities (PBS). These PBSs are responsible for distributing and managing electricity in their respective areas. As a result of this initiative, Bangladesh achieved nearly universal electrification, with over 99% of rural households having access to electricity.

De-centralized Renewable Energy Systems in Kenya: Kenya has implemented various decentralized renewable energy systems to improve rural electrification. One notable project is the Kenya Off-

Grid Solar Access Project (KOSAP), launched in 2018. KOSAP aims to provide clean energy access to over 1.1 million people in 14 underserved counties. The project supports the installation of solar mini-grids, solar home systems, and clean cooking solutions. By utilizing renewable energy sources, KOSAP has significantly improved access to electricity and enhanced livelihoods in rural communities.

Solar Electrification in Morocco: Morocco has implemented an ambitious rural electrification program utilizing solar energy. The Moroccan Agency for Sustainable Energy (MASEN) has been instrumental in deploying solar home systems in remote areas. The program aims to provide electricity access to 1 million households by 2025. By leveraging solar power, Morocco has overcome geographical challenges and provided sustainable electricity solutions to rural communities, contributing to economic development and improved living conditions.

The Barefoot College in India: The Barefoot College, located in Rajasthan, India, focuses on empowering rural communities through solar electrification. The college trains rural women, often illiterate or with minimal education, to become solar engineers, known as "Solar Mamas." These women learn to assemble, install, and maintain solar panels, providing electricity to their villages. This approach not only addresses the energy needs of rural communities but also empowers women by giving them valuable skills and income-generating opportunities.

These case studies highlight the diverse approaches taken by different countries to achieve rural electrification. They demonstrate the importance of tailored solutions, community involvement, and the utilization of renewable energy sources for sustainable and successful rural electrification projects.

CHAPTER 3

PLANNING AND PROJECT DEVELOPMENT

3.0 PLANNING AND PROJECT DEVELOPMENT FOR RURAL ELECTRIFICATION:

Planning and project development for rural

electrification involves a systematic approach to assess the energy needs, design appropriate solutions, secure financing, and implement the electrification project in rural areas. Here are the key steps involved in planning and project development for rural electrification:

3.1 Assessing energy needs and demand in rural communities:

Assessing energy needs and demand in rural communities is a crucial step in planning and development of rural electrification projects. It helps in understanding the specific energy requirements of the community and designing appropriate solutions to meet those needs. Here are some key considerations and approaches to assess energy needs and demand in rural areas:

Data Collection: Gather relevant data on the population, households, and economic activities in the target rural community. This includes demographic information, household size, types of businesses, agricultural practices, and other relevant factors. Collect information on existing energy sources and technologies used, such as traditional biomass, kerosene, or diesel generators. This can be done through surveys, interviews, census data, reports, and data collection from existing energy providers, local authorities, and community organizations.

Energy Consumption Analysis: Determine the current energy consumption patterns in the community. Identify the sources of energy being used, such as traditional fuels (like firewood, charcoal, kerosene) and any existing electricity access (if applicable). Quantify the amount of energy consumed for different purposes, such as lighting, cooking, heating, agriculture, and productive uses (e.g., small businesses, irrigation, processing).

Energy Access Gap Analysis: Identify the gap between the existing energy services and the desired energy access in the community. Assess the proportion of households, businesses, and institutions that currently lack access to electricity or rely on inadequate and unsustainable energy sources. This analysis helps in quantifying the scale of the electrification challenge and determining the target population for electrification interventions.

Future Demand Projections: Consider future growth and changes in the community to estimate the future energy demand. Factors such as population growth, urbanization, economic development, and technological advancements should be taken into account. Project the energy requirements for the medium to long term, considering potential changes in energy-consuming activities and the adoption of new technologies.

Productive Uses Assessment: Explore opportunities for productive uses of electricity that can contribute to income generation and economic development in the community. Identify existing and potential income-generating activities that could benefit from access to electricity, such as small-scale industries, agriculture processing, agribusinesses, and service enterprises. Assess the energy requirements and the potential impact of electrification on these activities.

Energy Efficiency Potential: Assess the potential for energy efficiency measures to optimize energy use in the community. Identify areas where energy-efficient technologies and practices can be implemented to reduce energy demand, improve energy access, and minimize operating costs. This may include promoting energy-efficient appliances, building insulation, efficient cooking stoves, and efficient water pumping and irrigation systems.

Technological and Infrastructure Considerations: Consider the technological options available for rural electrification, such as grid extension, mini-grid systems, or standalone renewable energy systems. Evaluate the suitability of each technology based on factors like resource availability, technical feasibility, affordability, and long-term sustainability. Assess the infrastructure requirements, including transmission and distribution lines, transformers, and equipment needed for each option.

Socio-economic Factors: Take into account the social and economic characteristics of the community, including income levels, affordability, education levels, and cultural aspects. Consider gender dynamics and the specific energy needs of women, as they often play a significant role in household energy-related activities. Incorporate social and cultural factors into the design of electrification solutions to ensure they are socially acceptable and sustainable.

Data Analysis and Documentation: Analyze the collected data and present the findings in a comprehensive report. Document the energy needs, demand projections, existing energy access gaps, potential opportunities, and challenges. This information will serve as a foundation for designing and implementing appropriate electrification solutions.

Cross-Verification and Validation: Cross-verify the data collected through different sources and approaches to ensure accuracy and reliability. Validate the findings by comparing them with existing energy data, conducting pilot studies, or seeking expert opinions.

Energy Audits: Conduct energy audits for specific sectors or facilities to identify opportunities for energy efficiency improvements. Assess the potential for energy-saving technologies, such as efficient lighting, appliances, and productive use equipment, to optimize energy consumption and reduce costs.

By conducting a thorough assessment of energy needs and demand in rural communities, planners and project developers can tailor electrification solutions to meet the specific requirements of the community, optimize resource allocation, ensure the long-term sustainability, effectiveness and aligned with the aspirations of the people they serve.

3.2 Stakeholder engagement and community participation:

Stakeholder engagement and community participation are integral to the success of rural electrification projects. Involving stakeholders and communities throughout the project lifecycle ensures that the electrification initiatives address their needs, are socially acceptable, and have long-term sustainability. Here are some key considerations for stakeholder engagement and community participation:

Identify Stakeholders: Identify and understand the various stakeholders involved in or affected by the electrification project. This includes community members, local leaders, government officials, NGOs, energy service providers, financial institutions, and other relevant actors. Consider the diversity of stakeholders and ensure the inclusion of marginalized groups, women, and youth.

Participatory Approach: Adopt a participatory approach that encourages active involvement and decision-making by stakeholders and the community. Create platforms for dialogue, information sharing, and collaborative decision-making. Ensure that all stakeholders have equal opportunities to express their views, raise concerns, and contribute to the project design and implementation.

Early Engagement: Initiate stakeholder engagement and community participation from the early stages of the project. Involve stakeholders in the project scoping, needs assessment, and feasibility study. Seek their inputs and feedback to ensure that the project aligns with their aspirations and priorities. Early engagement builds trust, fosters ownership, and increases the likelihood of project success.

Capacity Building: Provide capacity-building support to enhance the knowledge, skills, and understanding of stakeholders and the community. Conduct awareness programs, workshops, and training sessions to educate stakeholders about the benefits of electrification, energy-efficient practices, safety measures, and income-generating opportunities. Empower the community to actively participate in decision-making and take up roles in project implementation and maintenance.

Communication and Information Sharing: Establish effective communication channels to share project updates, progress, and outcomes with stakeholders and the community. Use various communication tools, such as community meetings, newsletters, social media, and local media outlets, to disseminate information in a clear and accessible manner. Encourage two-way communication to address concerns, clarify doubts, and gather feedback from stakeholders.

Community-Led Planning: Encourage community-led planning and decision-making processes. Facilitate the formation of local committees or task forces comprising community representatives who can actively participate in the project design, implementation, and monitoring. Enable the community to identify their energy needs, prioritize electrification interventions, and contribute to the development of customized solutions that fit their unique circumstances.

Benefit Sharing: Ensure that the benefits of rural electrification are shared equitably among the community. Define mechanisms for fair and transparent benefit distribution, such as affordable tariff structures, revenue-sharing models, or community-based ownership and management of electrification systems. Promote income-generating opportunities and support local entrepreneurship to create economic empowerment within the community.

Cultural Sensitivity: Respect and incorporate the cultural values, traditions, and norms of the community into the electrification project. Consider cultural practices related to energy use, gender roles, and community decision-making processes. Adapt project designs and approaches to align with local customs and preferences. Engage with community leaders and influencers to gain their support and ensure cultural acceptance.

Long-Term Engagement: Maintain a long-term engagement with stakeholders and the community even after the electrification project is implemented. Continue communication, provide support for capacity building, and involve stakeholders in project monitoring and evaluation. Foster a sense of ownership and sustainability by nurturing partnerships and networks that can support ongoing maintenance, operation, and future expansion of the electrification systems.

Stakeholder engagement and community participation are essential for creating a sense of ownership, ensuring project sustainability, and maximizing the socio-economic benefits of rural electrification. By involving stakeholders and communities as active partners, projects can better address local needs, build trust, and achieve long-term positive impacts.

3.3   Feasibility studies and site assessments:

Feasibility studies and site assessments are critical components of project planning and decision-making processes in various fields, including infrastructure development, energy projects, and construction. Let's explore each of them:

Feasibility Studies: Feasibility studies are conducted to assess the viability and potential success of a project before making significant investments. The primary objectives of feasibility studies include:

Assessing Technical Feasibility: Evaluating the technical aspects of the project, such as engineering design, technology requirements, and available resources. This analysis helps determine if the project can be implemented effectively.

Examining Economic Feasibility: Assessing the financial viability of the project, including cost estimation, revenue projections, return on investment (ROI), and potential risks. This analysis helps determine if the project is financially feasible and sustainable.

Analyzing Market Feasibility: Assessing the market demand, competition, and potential customers or beneficiaries of the project. This analysis helps determine if there is a viable market for the project's outputs or services.

Assessing Legal and Regulatory Feasibility: Examining legal and regulatory requirements, permits, licenses, and compliance obligations associated with the project. This analysis helps identify any potential legal barriers or constraints.

Evaluating Environmental and Social Feasibility: Assessing the potential environmental and social impacts of the project and identifying measures to mitigate any adverse effects. This analysis helps ensure the project aligns with environmental and social sustainability goals.

Feasibility studies provide decision-makers with valuable information to determine whether to proceed with a project, modify its scope, or abandon it based on the identified risks, costs, benefits, and market conditions.

Site Assessments:
Site assessments involve evaluating a specific location or site for a proposed project. The primary objectives of site assessments include:
Evaluating Physical Conditions: Assessing the physical characteristics of the site, including topography, soil conditions, geology, availability of natural resources, and any potential environmental constraints.

Analyzing Infrastructure and Access: Examining the existing infrastructure, transportation networks, utilities (such as water and electricity), and accessibility to the site. This analysis helps determine the suitability of the site for the intended project.

Identifying Risks and Constraints: Identifying potential risks, hazards, and constraints associated with the site, such as environmental risks, regulatory restrictions, land tenure issues, or cultural considerations. This analysis helps assess the overall suitability and feasibility of the site.

Considering Local Community and Stakeholder Factors: Assessing the social, economic, and cultural factors of the local community and stakeholders in the vicinity of the site. This analysis helps understand potential impacts and engagement strategies to ensure project acceptance and minimize conflicts.

Site assessments provide valuable insights into the specific characteristics and challenges of a location, enabling project planners and developers to make informed decisions regarding project design, implementation strategies, and mitigation measures.

Both feasibility studies and site assessments are essential in project planning and decision-making processes as they help identify risks, opportunities, and constraints. The findings and recommendations from these assessments provide a foundation for informed decision-making and increase the chances of project success.

Chukwujekwu John Okafor and Oko Obasi

CHAPTER 4

INFRASTRUCTURE DESIGN AND IMPLEMENT

Chukwujekwu John Okafor and Oko Obasi

INFRASTRUCTURE DESIGN AND IMPLEMENTATION

Infrastructure design and implementation are critical stages in rural electrification projects. Efficient and well-planned infrastructure ensures reliable and sustainable access to electricity in rural areas. Here are key considerations for infrastructure design and implementation:

4.1 Selection and design of power generation systems:

The selection and design of power generation systems for rural electrification projects depend on various factors, including resource availability, energy demand, budget, and local conditions. Here are some considerations for selecting and designing power generation systems:

Resource Assessment: Conduct a thorough assessment of the available resources in the target area. Determine the solar potential, wind speed, hydrological data, or any other relevant renewable energy resources. This assessment helps identify the most suitable renewable energy source for power generation.

Energy Demand: Estimate the energy demand of the rural area, considering the current and future requirements of households, businesses, and community facilities. Analyze load profiles, peak demand, and consumption patterns to determine the capacity of the power generation system.

Renewable Energy Options: Evaluate different renewable energy options based on resource availability and project requirements. Common options include solar photovoltaic (PV) systems, wind turbines, small hydropower systems, biomass power plants, or a combination of these sources. Consider the suitability of each option based on the resource availability, cost, scalability, and environmental impact.

System Size and Configuration: Determine the optimal size and configuration of the power generation system. This depends on the energy demand, resource availability, and project budget. For example, a standalone solar PV system can be designed for individual households, while a mini-grid system may be suitable for powering a cluster of households and community institutions.

Hybrid Systems: Consider hybrid power generation systems that combine multiple renewable energy sources. Hybrid systems can enhance reliability by utilizing complementary resources. For instance, combining solar PV and wind turbines can provide a more consistent power supply throughout the day and across seasons.

Storage Solutions: Assess the need for energy storage solutions, such as batteries, to ensure a continuous power supply. Energy storage systems can store excess energy during periods of high generation and discharge it during periods of low generation or peak demand. Battery storage can enhance system stability and enable power availability during nighttime or low-resource periods.

Grid Connectivity: Determine whether the project will connect to an existing grid or operate as an off-grid system. Grid extension may be feasible in areas with existing infrastructure, while off-grid systems, such as mini-grids or standalone systems, may be more suitable for remote regions. Consider the costs, transmission losses, and reliability associated with each option.

System Efficiency and Performance: Focus on designing an energy-efficient and reliable power generation system. Optimize the system components, including solar panels, wind turbines, inverters, or generators, to maximize energy conversion and minimize losses. Consider the use of high-quality equipment and ensure adherence to technical standards and regulations.

Environmental Impact: Evaluate the environmental impact of the power generation system. Renewable energy sources have relatively low environmental impact compared to fossil fuel-based systems. However, it's important to consider factors such as land use, ecosystem conservation, noise pollution, and visual aesthetics during the design process.

Lifecycle Cost Analysis: Perform a comprehensive lifecycle cost analysis, considering the upfront investment, operation, and maintenance costs. Compare different power generation options to assess the long-term financial viability and payback period. Include factors such as fuel costs, maintenance requirements, and potential revenue streams to estimate the overall project economics.

The selection and design of power generation systems should be based on a holistic analysis of technical, economic, environmental, and social factors. Engaging with experts, renewable energy specialists, and local stakeholders can provide valuable insights and ensure that the chosen power generation system aligns with the specific needs and conditions of the rural electrification project.

Chukwujekwu John Okafor and Oko Obasi

4.2 Distribution network planning and grid extension strategies:

Distribution network planning and grid extension strategies are essential for rural electrification projects to ensure reliable and efficient delivery of electricity to end consumers. Here are key considerations for distribution network planning and grid extension strategies:

Load Analysis: Conduct a thorough analysis of the projected energy demand and load patterns in the target area. This includes assessing the number of households, businesses, and community institutions that will be connected to the grid. Understand the peak demand, average consumption, and load growth projections to determine the required capacity and infrastructure design.

Geographic Mapping: Map the target area to understand the geographical layout, population density, and distribution of potential consumers. Identify areas with high electricity demand concentration and those with dispersed consumer clusters. This information helps determine the optimal routing and configuration of the distribution network.

Grid Extension vs. Standalone Systems: Evaluate

whether grid extension or standalone systems (mini-grids or individual systems) are more appropriate for the target area. Grid extension is suitable when the population density is high, and the cost of connecting to the main grid is justified. Standalone systems are cost-effective for remote areas with low population density or where grid access is challenging.

Technical Design: Determine the technical parameters of the distribution network, including the voltage level, conductor size, and transformer capacity. Consider factors such as power losses, voltage regulation, and reliability when designing the network. Utilize computer-aided design tools to simulate and optimize the network configuration.

Distribution Line Routing: Plan the routing of distribution lines based on factors such as terrain, accessibility, and cost-efficiency. Minimize the length of distribution lines, considering the topography and vegetation to reduce installation and maintenance challenges. Prioritize routes that minimize environmental impact and land acquisition requirements.

Transformer Placement: Determine the optimal locations for distribution transformers to ensure efficient voltage regulation and minimize energy losses. Consider load density, distance from the grid connection point, and voltage drop constraints when placing transformers. Transformer sizing should align with the expected load demand and future expansion needs.

System Protection and Safety: Implement appropriate protection mechanisms to ensure the safety of the distribution network and connected consumers. This includes installing protective devices such as fuses, circuit breakers, and surge suppressors. Conduct fault analysis and design the system to minimize the impact of faults on power supply reliability.

Metering and Billing: Plan the installation of meters at consumer premises to accurately measure electricity consumption. Consider options such as prepaid meters, smart meters, or traditional postpaid meters based on the technical requirements and the availability of communication infrastructure. Design a billing system that is transparent, efficient, and tailored to the needs of the consumers.

Maintenance and Asset Management: Develop a comprehensive maintenance and asset management plan for the distribution network. This includes regular inspection, maintenance, and repair of equipment, as well as vegetation management along distribution lines. Implement an asset management system to track the condition of assets, plan replacements, and optimize maintenance schedules.

Community Engagement: Involve the local community in the distribution network planning process. Seek their input, address their concerns, and provide information about the benefits and responsibilities associated with grid extension. Community engagement fosters a sense of ownership, promotes acceptance of the project, and facilitates smooth implementation.

Grid extension and distribution network planning require collaboration among various stakeholders, including government agencies, energy providers, technical experts, and local communities. Engaging experienced engineers, distribution planners, and local stakeholders can help ensure that the network design and grid extension strategies are tailored to the specific needs of the rural electrification project.

4.3   Off-grid solutions: Mini-grids and standalone systems:

Off-grid solutions, such as mini-grids and standalone systems, play a crucial role in rural electrification, particularly in areas where grid extension is not feasible or economically viable. These decentralized solutions provide electricity to communities that are geographically isolated or located far from existing power infrastructure. Here's an overview of mini-grids and standalone systems:

Mini-grids: Mini-grids are localized electricity distribution systems that generate and distribute electricity to a specific area or community. They consist of a combination of power generation sources (typically renewable energy-based) and a distribution network.

Power Generation: Mini-grids often integrate renewable energy sources like solar PV, wind turbines, small hydro, or biomass. Diesel generators can also be used as backup or for periods of high demand.

Distribution Network: Mini-grids have a distribution network that includes power lines, transformers, control systems, and meters to supply electricity to individual consumers.

Community Ownership: Mini-grids can be community-owned and managed, with local entities or cooperatives responsible for the operation, maintenance, and revenue collection. This fosters local entrepreneurship and promotes community participation.

Scalability: Mini-grids can be designed to cater to the specific energy needs of a community, and they can be scaled up or expanded as the demand grows. They provide flexibility in terms of capacity and can support productive uses of electricity for local businesses and income generation.

Standalone Systems: Standalone systems, also known as individual or pico solar systems, are independent electricity systems that provide power to a single household or a small group of users. These systems are typically powered by solar energy and include a solar panel, battery storage, and energy-efficient appliances.

Solar Home Systems (SHS): SHS are standalone solar systems designed for residential use. They typically consist of a solar panel, battery storage, charge controller, and lighting fixtures. SHS can power small appliances like mobile phone chargers, radios, and fans, improving household lighting and basic electricity access.

Micro-grids: In some cases, multiple standalone systems can be interconnected to form a micro-grid, which serves a small cluster of buildings or households. Micro-grids may have a shared battery storage system and can support slightly higher loads and additional appliances.

Portability and Affordability: Standalone systems are portable, easy to install, and can be owned by individual households. They provide an affordable and accessible option for households in remote areas that are not connected to the main grid.

Pay-as-you-go (PAYG) Models: Standalone systems are often deployed using PAYG models, where users pay for electricity on a pay-as-you-go basis using mobile money or other payment systems. This enables greater affordability and flexibility for households with limited financial resources.

Both mini-grids and standalone systems offer viable solutions for rural electrification by providing access to clean, reliable, and affordable electricity. The choice between these options depends on factors such as community size, energy demand, available renewable energy resources, affordability, and local preferences. The selection of the most appropriate off-grid solution should be based on a thorough assessment of the specific needs and context of the target community.

4.4   Integration of renewable energy sources:

Chukwujekwu John Okafor and Oko Obasi

The integration of renewable energy sources is a key aspect of rural electrification, as it promotes sustainability, reduces reliance on fossil fuels, and contributes to mitigating climate change. Here are some important considerations for the integration of renewable energy sources in rural electrification:

Resource Assessment: Conduct a thorough assessment of renewable energy resources available in the target area. This includes solar, wind, hydro, biomass, or geothermal potential. Analyze historical data, conduct on-site measurements, or use satellite data to determine the energy potential and feasibility of different renewable sources.

Technological Selection: Choose the most suitable renewable energy technologies based on the available resources, energy demand, and project objectives. Solar photovoltaic (PV) systems are commonly used for decentralized electrification, while wind turbines or micro-hydro systems can be suitable in areas with high wind or water resources. Biomass or biogas systems may be appropriate if there is sufficient organic waste available for fuel.

Hybrid Systems: Consider the use of hybrid systems that combine multiple renewable energy sources to enhance reliability and optimize generation. Integrating different renewable sources, such as solar and wind, with complementary generation profiles can ensure a more stable and consistent power supply. Battery storage systems can also be incorporated to store excess energy for use during periods of low renewable generation.

System Design and Sizing: Design the renewable energy system to meet the specific energy needs of the community. Consider factors such as peak demand, load profiles, and seasonal variations in energy consumption. Conduct detailed energy modeling and simulation to determine the appropriate system size, number of panels or turbines, battery capacity, and inverters. This ensures efficient utilization of renewable energy resources.

Grid Integration: If the project involves grid-connected rural electrification, design the system to integrate renewable energy sources with the existing grid infrastructure. Ensure compatibility with grid standards, grid stability, and power quality requirements. Explore mechanisms such as net metering, feed-in tariffs, or power purchase agreements to incentivize the integration of renewable energy into the grid.

Energy Storage: Incorporate energy storage systems, such as batteries, into the renewable energy system to provide continuous power supply and address intermittency issues. Battery storage allows for the storage of excess energy generated during periods of high renewable generation and its utilization during periods of low or no generation. This improves reliability and enables the use of renewable energy even during non-sunlight or low-wind periods.

Grid Management and Control: Implement advanced monitoring, control, and management systems to optimize the performance of the renewable energy system. This includes real-time monitoring of energy generation, load demand, and battery status. Implement intelligent control algorithms to balance generation and demand, maximize renewable energy utilization, and ensure stability in the system.

Local Capacity Building: Provide training and capacity-building programs for local technicians and operators to ensure the proper operation and maintenance of the renewable energy system. This empowers the local community to take ownership of the system, perform routine maintenance, and troubleshoot common issues. Local capacity building contributes to the sustainability and long-term viability of the renewable energy project.

Economic Viability: Assess the economic viability of the renewable energy system by considering the lifecycle costs, including installation, operation, and maintenance. Compare the costs with alternative energy sources and analyze the long-term financial benefits, such as reduced fuel costs and potential income generation from productive use of electricity. Explore financing mechanisms, subsidies, or grants to make renewable energy solutions more affordable and financially sustainable.

Environmental and Social Impact: Consider the environmental and social impact of the renewable energy system. Ensure that the project adheres to environmental regulations and standards. Minimize potential negative impacts on ecosystems, wildlife, and local communities. Engage with stakeholders and the community to raise awareness, address concerns, and maximize the social benefits of the renewable energy project.

The integration of renewable energy sources in rural electrification projects can provide clean, reliable, and sustainable electricity access to rural communities. By leveraging renewable energy technologies and considering the specific local context, electrification initiatives can contribute to sustainable development, energy security, and environmental conservation.

4.5 Energy storage solutions for rural electrification:

Energy storage solutions play a crucial role in rural electrification by addressing the intermittent nature of renewable energy sources and ensuring reliable and continuous power supply. Here are some commonly used Energy storage technologies for rural electrification:

Battery Energy Storage Systems (BESS):

a) Lead-Acid Batteries: Lead-acid batteries are a mature and widely used technology for energy storage. They are relatively low-cost and have good cycling capabilities. However, they have lower energy density and shorter lifespan compared to other technologies.

b) Lithium-Ion Batteries: Lithium-ion batteries have gained popularity due to their high energy density, longer lifespan, and better cycling capabilities. They offer faster charging and discharging rates and are suitable for a wide range of applications. Lithium-ion batteries are commonly used in solar home systems, mini-grids, and hybrid renewable energy systems.

c)Flow Batteries: Flow batteries, such as vanadium redox flow batteries (VRFB), store energy in liquid electrolytes. They offer long cycle life and can be easily scaled up for large-scale energy storage applications. Flow batteries are suitable for longer-duration storage needs and can provide continuous power for extended periods.

Pumped Hydro Storage: Pumped hydro storage is a well-established and efficient method of energy storage. It involves pumping water from a lower reservoir to an upper reservoir when there is excess electricity generation, and then releasing it back down through turbines to generate electricity when there is high demand. This technology requires suitable geographical features, such as hilly terrain and access to water bodies.

Compressed Air Energy Storage (CAES): CAES systems store energy by compressing air into underground caverns or storage vessels. During peak demand, the compressed air is released and expanded through turbines to generate electricity. CAES can provide longer-duration storage and can be combined with renewable energy sources to provide a stable power supply.

Flywheel Energy Storage: Flywheel energy storage systems store energy in a rotating mass, typically made of a high-speed rotor. Excess electricity is used to accelerate the rotor, and when electricity is needed, the rotational energy is converted back to electricity. Flywheel systems provide fast response times, high power output, and are suitable for applications that require short-duration storage and frequent charge-discharge cycles.

Thermal Energy Storage: Thermal energy storage systems store excess energy in the form of heat or cold. This energy can be used later for heating, cooling, or electricity generation. Examples of thermal energy storage include using phase change materials (PCMs) or storing heat in molten salts.

The choice of energy storage solution depends on various factors such as the required storage capacity, duration of storage, power output, cost, available resources, and project-specific requirements. In rural electrification projects, a combination of battery energy storage systems and other technologies like pumped hydro storage or thermal energy storage can be employed to provide reliable and sustainable electricity access to remote communities.

It's important to note that advancements in energy storage technologies are continually being made, and new solutions may emerge in the future, offering even more options for rural electrification.

4.6 Safety standards and regulations in rural electrification:

Safety standards and regulations play a critical role in ensuring the safe design, installation, operation, and maintenance of rural electrification systems. They help protect the well-being of individuals, prevent accidents, and maintain the reliability and longevity of the electrical infrastructure. Here are some key aspects of safety standards and regulations in rural electrification:

National Electrical Codes and Standards: Most countries have national electrical codes and standards that provide guidelines for the safe installation and operation of electrical systems. These codes outline requirements for wiring, grounding, protection devices, and other aspects of electrical infrastructure. Compliance with these codes is essential to ensure the safety and reliability of rural electrification projects.

Equipment Standards and Certifications: Electrical equipment used in rural electrification, such as solar panels, batteries, inverters, and distribution components, should adhere to recognized standards and certifications. These standards ensure that the equipment meets minimum safety requirements, has been tested for performance, and complies with relevant technical specifications.

Safety Training and Education: It is crucial to provide safety training and education to all stakeholders involved in rural electrification, including project developers, installers, maintenance personnel, and end-users. Training programs should cover topics such as electrical safety practices, equipment handling, emergency response procedures, and proper use of electrical appliances. Promoting awareness and knowledge about electrical safety helps prevent accidents and promotes safe practices in rural electrification.

System Design and Installation: Safety considerations should be incorporated into the design and installation of rural electrification systems. This includes proper sizing of components, correct wiring practices, appropriate grounding techniques, and adherence to safety distances and clearances. Following best practices in system design and installation minimizes the risk of electrical hazards and ensures reliable and safe operation.

Electrical Inspections and Audits: Regular inspections and audits should be conducted to assess the safety and compliance of rural electrification systems. This involves reviewing the installation, assessing the condition of equipment, and identifying any potential safety issues or non-compliance with regulations. Inspections help identify and rectify safety hazards, ensuring the continued safety and reliability of the electrical infrastructure.

Protection against Electric Shock and Fire Hazards: Safety measures such as proper grounding, circuit protection devices (such as fuses and circuit breakers), and insulation are essential to protect against electric shock and fire hazards. Implementing appropriate protection measures, including residual current devices (RCDs) or ground fault circuit interrupters (GFCIs), enhances safety by quickly detecting and interrupting faulty electrical circuits.

Community Awareness and Safety Campaigns: Engaging the local community and raising awareness about electrical safety is crucial. Conduct safety campaigns, workshops, and awareness programs to educate community members about potential electrical hazards, safe usage of electricity, and actions to take in case of emergencies. Empowering the community with knowledge promotes a culture of safety and reduces the risk of accidents.

Ongoing Maintenance and System Upkeep: Regular maintenance of rural electrification systems is essential for safety. This includes periodic inspection of equipment, cleaning solar panels, testing and replacing batteries, and ensuring proper functioning of protection devices. Scheduled maintenance helps identify and address any safety issues, preventing potential accidents and ensuring the long-term reliability of the system.

Regulatory Oversight and Enforcement: Effective regulatory oversight is necessary to enforce safety standards and regulations in rural electrification projects. Regulatory bodies should monitor compliance, conduct inspections, and take appropriate actions against non-compliant installations or practices. Clear enforcement mechanisms and penalties for non-compliance create accountability and promote adherence to safety standards.

It is important to note that safety standards and regulations may vary across different countries and regions. Therefore, it is essential to comply with the specific requirements and guidelines set by the relevant authorities in the respective jurisdiction where the rural electrification project is being implemented.

CHAPTER 5

OPERATION, MAINTENANCE AND SUSTAINABILITY

5.1 Establishing efficient operation and maintenance protocols:

Establishing efficient operation and maintenance protocols is crucial for ensuring the long-term reliability, performance, and sustainability of rural electrification projects. Here are key steps and considerations for developing effective operation and maintenance (O&M) protocols:

Asset Inventory and Management: Begin by creating

a comprehensive inventory of all assets within the electrification system. This includes power generation equipment, distribution infrastructure, transformers, meters, control systems, and any other components. Implement an asset management system to track the condition, maintenance history, and lifecycle of each asset.

Maintenance Planning: Develop a structured maintenance plan that outlines regular maintenance activities, inspection schedules, and preventive maintenance tasks. Consider the manufacturer's recommendations, industry best practices, and regulatory requirements when planning maintenance activities. Determine the frequency of maintenance based on asset type, usage patterns, and environmental conditions.

Skilled Workforce: Ensure that there is a skilled workforce available to perform maintenance tasks. Train and empower local technicians and operators to handle routine maintenance activities and minor repairs. Collaborate with local training institutions or organizations to provide specialized training on specific equipment or systems.

Monitoring and Performance Evaluation: Implement a monitoring system to track the performance of the electrification system. This may include real-time monitoring of energy generation, distribution parameters, voltage levels, and consumption patterns. Regularly analyze the collected data to identify performance issues, detect faults, and optimize system efficiency.

Reactive Maintenance: Develop protocols for addressing unexpected breakdowns or faults. Establish a responsive mechanism for reporting and addressing consumer complaints or service interruptions. Implement a structured system for prioritizing and addressing reactive maintenance tasks promptly to minimize downtime and customer inconvenience.

Spare Parts and Inventory Management: Maintain an inventory of critical spare parts and consumables necessary for maintenance activities. Ensure that the inventory is regularly updated, and there is a reliable supply chain for procuring necessary parts. Implement efficient inventory management practices to minimize stockouts and ensure timely availability of required items.

Safety and Compliance: Prioritize safety protocols to protect both maintenance personnel and end consumers. Ensure that maintenance activities comply with applicable safety regulations, electrical codes, and industry standards. Provide appropriate personal protective equipment (PPE) and safety training to maintenance staff.

Documentation and Reporting: Establish a system for documenting maintenance activities, including work orders, service reports, and maintenance logs. Maintain records of maintenance schedules, tasks performed, and any repairs or replacements made. Regularly review and analyze maintenance records to identify trends, recurring issues, and opportunities for improvement.

Collaboration and Partnerships: Collaborate with equipment suppliers, manufacturers, and technical experts to access technical support, training, and guidance on maintenance practices. Explore partnerships with local service providers, maintenance contractors, or neighboring electrification projects to share resources, knowledge, and experiences.

Continuous Improvement: Foster a culture of continuous improvement by regularly evaluating and optimizing maintenance protocols. Solicit feedback from maintenance staff, consumers, and other stakeholders to identify areas for improvement. Encourage innovation, knowledge sharing, and the adoption of new technologies or approaches to enhance the efficiency and effectiveness of maintenance activities.

Regularly review and update the O&M protocols based on feedback, performance evaluations, and emerging industry practices. By establishing efficient operation and maintenance protocols, rural electrification projects can ensure the longevity, reliability, and optimal performance of the electrification infrastructure.

5.2 Training local technicians and community members:

Training local technicians and community members is a crucial component of rural electrification projects. It helps build local capacity, empowers individuals with technical skills, and promotes sustainable development within the community. Here are some considerations for training local technicians and community members in rural electrification:

Needs Assessment: Conduct a needs assessment to identify the specific skills and knowledge required for the rural electrification project. Assess the existing technical capacity within the community and identify gaps that need to be addressed through training. This assessment will help tailor the training programs to the specific needs and context of the community.

Technical Training Programs: Develop comprehensive training programs that cover the technical aspects of rural electrification. These programs should include topics such as system design, installation, operation, maintenance, troubleshooting, and safety practices. The training can be delivered through a combination of classroom sessions, practical hands-on exercises, and field demonstrations.

Training of Trainers (ToT): Identify and train a core group of individuals from the community who can become trainers themselves. These individuals should have a strong technical background and the ability to effectively transfer their knowledge to others. Conduct ToT programs to equip them with the necessary training skills and techniques to deliver training to local technicians and community members.

Practical Hands-on Experience: Emphasize practical training and hands-on experience to enhance the participants' understanding and skills. Provide opportunities for trainees to work on real-world installations, conduct maintenance tasks, and troubleshoot common issues. Practical experience helps build confidence and ensures that trainees are well-prepared for the actual implementation and operation of rural electrification systems.

Community Engagement: Involve the local community in the training process. Seek their input, involvement, and active participation. This creates a sense of ownership and ensures that the training programs align with the community's needs and aspirations. Encourage community members to participate in training sessions, ask questions, and share their experiences, fostering a collaborative learning environment.

Language and Cultural Sensitivity: Consider language and cultural factors when designing the training programs. Ensure that the training materials are available in the local language or in a language that the participants are comfortable with. Adapt the training content to be culturally sensitive, taking into account local practices, customs, and norms.

Continuous Support and Mentorship: Establish mechanisms for ongoing support and mentorship for the trained technicians and community members. Provide access to technical resources, manuals, and guidelines that they can refer to after the training. Foster a network or community of practice where participants can seek advice, share experiences, and continue learning from each other.

Entrepreneurship and Business Skills: In addition to technical training, consider incorporating entrepreneurship and business skills training for those interested in offering services related to rural electrification. This includes topics such as business management, financial planning, marketing, and customer relations. Equipping individuals with entrepreneurial skills can help create local businesses and income-generating opportunities in the electrification sector.

Monitoring and Evaluation: Implement a monitoring and evaluation system to assess the effectiveness of the training programs. Collect feedback from participants to continuously improve the training content, delivery methods, and overall impact. Monitor the performance and progress of trained technicians and community members to identify areas for additional support or advanced training.

Sustainability and Long-term Support: Ensure that the training programs have a long-term perspective and are supported by adequate resources. Consider mechanisms for ongoing support, refresher training, and knowledge sharing. Collaborate with local institutions, NGOs, or government agencies to sustain the training initiatives and integrate them into broader skill development programs.

Training local technicians and community members not only builds technical capacity but also fosters economic empowerment, local entrepreneurship, and a sense of ownership within the community. It contributes to the sustainability and long-term success of rural electrification projects by creating a skilled workforce that can operate, maintain, and expand the electrification infrastructure.

5.3 Ensuring reliable electricity supply and troubleshooting:

Ensuring reliable electricity supply and effectively troubleshooting any issues that arise are crucial for maintaining uninterrupted power and resolving problems promptly. Here are some key steps and strategies for ensuring reliable electricity supply and troubleshooting:

Robust Infrastructure and Maintenance:
1. Invest in reliable and well-maintained electricity infrastructure, including power generation, transmission, and distribution systems.
2.Regularly inspect and maintain equipment, ensuring proper functioning and addressing any potential issues proactively.
3.Implement preventive maintenance schedules and

follow industry best practices to minimize downtime and extend equipment lifespan.

Monitoring and Remote Management:

1.Utilize advanced monitoring systems and remote management technologies to continuously monitor the performance of the electricity infrastructure.

2.Collect real-time data on voltage levels, load patterns, equipment status, and other relevant parameters to detect abnormalities and identify potential issues.

3.Implement automated alert systems to promptly notify responsible personnel when deviations or anomalies occur.

Redundancy and Backup Systems:

1.Establish redundancy measures, such as backup power sources (e.g., generators, battery storage) and redundant transmission or distribution lines.

2.Implement automatic or manual switchovers to backup systems in case of primary system failures.

3.Regularly test and maintain backup systems to ensure they are fully functional when needed.

Proactive Load Management:

1.Monitor and manage electricity demand to avoid overloading the system and minimize the risk of outages.

2.Implement load shedding or demand response

mechanisms to balance the power supply and demand during peak periods or emergencies.

3.Encourage energy efficiency practices among consumers to reduce overall load on the system.

Rapid Response and Troubleshooting:

1.Establish a well-defined process for reporting and responding to power-related issues, including power outages or equipment failures.

2.Maintain a skilled and trained workforce capable of quickly diagnosing and troubleshooting problems.

3.Have a clear escalation path and communication channels to coordinate efforts among various stakeholders, including field technicians, engineers, and relevant authorities.

Customer Support and Communication:

1.Maintain a responsive and efficient customer support system to address electricity-related complaints and inquiries promptly.

2.Establish clear communication channels to notify customers about planned outages, maintenance schedules, and any unforeseen disruptions.

3.Provide regular updates on the progress of issue resolution, estimated restoration times, and any necessary safety precautions.

Continuous Improvement and System Upgrades:

1.Regularly assess the performance and reliability of the electricity supply system and identify areas for improvement.

2.Invest in system upgrades, technology advancements, and modernization efforts to enhance the reliability, efficiency, and resilience of the electrical infrastructure.

3.Stay informed about industry trends, new technologies, and best practices to proactively address potential challenges and leverage opportunities for improvement.

Remember that ensuring reliable electricity supply is an ongoing process that requires proactive monitoring, regular maintenance, and continuous improvement efforts. By implementing robust infrastructure, proactive maintenance practices, advanced monitoring systems, backup solutions, and effective troubleshooting procedures, you can minimize disruptions and deliver reliable electricity services to customers.

5.4 Tariff models and revenue collection strategies:

Tariff models and revenue collection strategies are essential for ensuring the financial sustainability of rural electrification projects. Here are some commonly used approaches:

Chukwujekwu John Okafor and Oko Obasi

TARIFF:

i)Flat Tariff: This is a simple and straightforward tariff structure where all consumers are charged a fixed rate per unit of electricity consumed. It is easy to understand and administer but may not take into account variations in energy consumption or the ability to pay among different consumer groups.

ii)Tiered Tariff: A tiered tariff structure involves different pricing tiers based on energy consumption levels. The tariff increases as consumers move to higher consumption tiers. This model encourages efficient energy use and ensures that higher energy consumers pay more. It can be particularly useful in rural electrification projects where there may be significant variations in energy usage among consumers.

iii)Time-of-Use (TOU) Tariff: TOU tariffs vary the electricity price based on different time periods. Electricity is priced higher during peak demand periods and lower during off-peak hours. TOU tariffs can incentivize consumers to shift their electricity usage to off-peak hours, which helps balance the load and optimize the use of available electricity supply.

iv)Demand-Based Tariff: In this model, consumers

are charged based on their peak demand rather than energy consumption. It encourages consumers to manage their peak demand and can be suitable for consumers with high intermittent loads, such as small businesses or agricultural operations. However, it requires the installation of appropriate metering and monitoring systems to measure peak demand accurately.

V)Subsidized Tariff: In some cases, governments or funding agencies may provide subsidies to make electricity more affordable for rural communities. Subsidies can be targeted towards specific consumer groups, such as low-income households or productive use customers. This ensures that electricity remains affordable while still providing a revenue stream for the electrification project.

vi)Prepaid Metering: Prepaid metering systems require consumers to pay for electricity in advance by purchasing tokens or credits. This system allows consumers to manage their electricity usage and expenses more effectively. Prepaid metering can be combined with different tariff models to ensure revenue collection and promote efficient energy use.

Revenue Collection Strategies: To ensure effective revenue collection, consider the following strategies:

1.Establish clear billing and payment procedures and communicate them to consumers.
2.Use reliable metering systems to accurately measure energy consumption.
3.Implement a robust billing and collection system, including meter reading, invoicing, and payment tracking.
4.Provide multiple payment options, such as mobile money, bank transfers, or payment agents, to cater to different consumer preferences and improve accessibility.
5.Strengthen the capacity of the local utility or community-based organization to manage billing and revenue collection processes effectively.
6.Conduct regular monitoring and follow-up on outstanding payments to minimize revenue losses.
7.Implement penalties or incentives for timely payment to encourage compliance and prompt revenue collection.
8.Consider partnerships with local financial institutions or mobile network operators to facilitate convenient payment options and increase the efficiency of revenue collection.

It is important to strike a balance between affordability for consumers and generating sufficient revenue to cover operational and maintenance costs, as well as future investments in the electrification infrastructure. Tariff models and revenue collection strategies should be tailored to the local context, taking into account the income levels, energy consumption patterns, and affordability of the rural population. Regular review and adjustments may be necessary to ensure the financial sustainability of the electrification project.

5.5 Evaluating and optimizing system performance:

Evaluating and optimizing system performance is essential for ensuring the effectiveness and efficiency of rural electrification projects. Here are key steps and considerations for evaluating and optimizing system performance:

Performance Metrics: Define key performance metrics to assess the effectiveness of the electrification system. These metrics may include energy availability, system reliability, voltage stability, power quality, customer satisfaction, and financial performance. Establish benchmarks and targets for each metric to track progress and identify areas for improvement.

Data Collection and Analysis: Implement a data collection system to gather relevant performance data. This may involve monitoring energy generation, distribution parameters, customer feedback, outage records, and maintenance logs. Analyze the collected data to identify trends, patterns, and performance gaps. Utilize data analytics tools to gain insights and make data-driven decisions.

Performance Evaluation: Regularly evaluate system performance against the defined metrics and benchmarks. Conduct periodic assessments to measure energy losses, system downtime, voltage fluctuations, and other relevant indicators. Compare actual performance with the established targets and identify areas where improvements can be made.

Root Cause Analysis: When performance issues or gaps are identified, conduct root cause analysis to determine the underlying factors contributing to the problem. Investigate the causes of outages, voltage instability, or low energy availability. Consider technical, operational, and management aspects that may impact system performance. This analysis helps identify the specific areas that require attention and improvement.

Optimization Strategies: Based on the findings from the performance evaluation and root cause analysis, develop optimization strategies to address identified issues. This may involve implementing corrective actions such as equipment upgrades, network reconfiguration, maintenance process improvements, or system redesign. Prioritize the strategies based on their potential impact on system performance and feasibility of implementation.

Load Management and Demand-Side Measures: Explore demand-side management strategies to optimize system performance. This includes promoting energy efficiency practices, load shifting, and demand response programs. Educate consumers on efficient energy use and incentivize them to modify their consumption patterns to align with system capabilities and peak demand periods.

System Upgrades and Expansions: Assess the need for system upgrades or expansions based on the performance evaluation and future demand projections. Determine whether additional generation capacity, distribution infrastructure, or storage solutions are required to meet the growing energy demand. Evaluate the cost-effectiveness and environmental impact of proposed upgrades or expansions.

Stakeholder Engagement: Engage with stakeholders, including consumers, local communities, technical experts, and relevant authorities, to gather feedback and insights on system performance. Seek their input on potential areas for improvement and innovative solutions. Encourage participation and collaboration to ensure that optimization efforts align with the needs and aspirations of the stakeholders.

Performance Monitoring and Reporting: Continuously monitor and track the implemented optimization strategies to assess their effectiveness. Establish a reporting mechanism to communicate system performance and improvement initiatives to stakeholders. Transparently share performance results, achievements, and challenges to build trust and accountability among stakeholders.

Continuous Learning and Adaptation: Foster a culture of continuous learning and adaptation within the electrification project. Encourage knowledge sharing, capacity building, and the adoption of best practices. Stay updated with emerging technologies, industry trends, and regulatory changes that may impact system performance. Continuously refine and adjust optimization strategies based on new insights and lessons learned.

By evaluating and optimizing system performance,

rural electrification projects can enhance energy availability, reliability, and customer satisfaction. The iterative process of evaluation, analysis, and improvement ensures that the electrification system evolves to meet the changing needs of the rural community.

5.6 Sustainability and long-term viability of rural electrification projects: Ensuring the sustainability and long-term viability of rural electrification projects is essential to maximize their impact and benefits. Here are some key considerations to promote sustainability in rural electrification projects:

Renewable Energy Sources: Emphasize the use of renewable energy sources such as solar, wind, hydro, biomass, or geothermal energy. These sources reduce reliance on fossil fuels, mitigate environmental impacts, and provide a sustainable and clean energy solution.

Energy Efficiency: Promote energy-efficient practices and technologies to optimize energy use and reduce waste. This can include promoting efficient appliances, energy-saving practices, and educating the community on energy conservation.

Community Engagement and Capacity Building:

Involve the local community in the project planning, implementation, and decision-making processes. Engage community members through awareness campaigns, training programs, and capacity-building initiatives to develop their understanding of the technology, maintenance, and operation of the electrification system.

Financial Sustainability: Develop a financially sustainable model for the electrification project. Consider factors such as revenue collection mechanisms, cost recovery strategies, tariff structures, and potential income-generating activities linked to electricity access. Explore innovative financing models, public-private partnerships, or community-based ownership structures to ensure the financial viability of the project.

Operation and Maintenance: Establish a robust operation and maintenance framework for the electrification infrastructure. Regular inspections, maintenance schedules, and skilled workforce training are essential to keep the system running efficiently and minimize downtime. Engage local technicians or provide training opportunities to ensure the availability of skilled personnel for maintenance tasks.

Monitoring and Evaluation: Implement monitoring and evaluation mechanisms to assess the project's performance and impact over time. Regularly measure key performance indicators such as energy generation, access levels, reliability, customer satisfaction, and environmental impact. Use this information to identify areas for improvement and make informed decisions for project optimization.

Policy and Regulatory Support: Advocate for supportive policies and regulations that encourage rural electrification and renewable energy development. Seek governmental support in terms of policy incentives, subsidies, and favorable regulatory frameworks to facilitate project implementation and sustainability.

Partnerships and Collaboration: Foster partnerships with local stakeholders, government agencies, NGOs, private sector entities, and international organizations. Collaboration can enhance technical expertise, resource mobilization, knowledge sharing, and community engagement efforts, thereby contributing to the sustainability of the project.

Long-Term Planning and Adaptability: Incorporate long-term planning into project design, considering future energy needs, technological advancements, and changing community requirements. Build flexibility into the system design to accommodate future expansion, upgrades, or integration of new technologies.

Environmental and Social Impact Assessment: Conduct thorough environmental and social impact assessments to identify potential risks and mitigation measures. Ensure the project aligns with environmental sustainability goals, cultural sensitivities, and social well-being of the local community.

By integrating these considerations into the project design, implementation, and management processes, rural electrification projects can be developed in a manner that maximizes sustainability, long-term viability, and positive impact on the community and the environment.

Chukwujekwu John Okafor and Oko Obasi

CHAPTER 6

SOCIO-ECONOMIC AND COMMUNITY DEVELOPMENT

6.1   Socio-economic   benefits   of   rural

electrification:

Rural electrification brings numerous socio-economic benefits to communities, contributing to their overall development and well-being. Here are some key socio-economic benefits of rural electrification:

Improved Quality of Life: Access to electricity enhances the quality of life for rural communities. It enables the use of electric lighting, improving visibility and extending productive hours. It also facilitates access to modern amenities like refrigeration, electric cooking appliances, and clean water supply, leading to improved health, nutrition, and overall living conditions.

Enhanced Education and Communication: Electricity enables the use of electronic devices such as computers, laptops, and tablets, providing opportunities for e-learning, digital literacy, and access to online educational resources. It also enables the establishment of telecommunication infrastructure, allowing better connectivity, access to information, and improved communication channels within and outside the community.

Economic Productivity and Entrepreneurship: Rural electrification opens up opportunities for economic growth and entrepreneurship. With access to electricity, rural communities can engage in income-generating activities, such as small-scale industries, agriculture processing, and local businesses. Electric-powered machinery and equipment can boost productivity and efficiency, leading to increased incomes and job creation.

Agricultural Development: Electricity facilitates the adoption of modern agricultural practices, such as irrigation systems, mechanization, and agro-processing equipment. Electric-powered tools and machinery improve agricultural productivity, crop yields, and post-harvest processing. Access to electricity also enables the use of refrigeration for storage, reducing post-harvest losses and increasing market opportunities for farmers.

Access to Healthcare Services: Electricity plays a crucial role in healthcare delivery. It powers medical equipment, refrigeration for vaccines and medications, lighting for clinics and hospitals, and facilitates telemedicine services. Access to electricity in rural areas improves healthcare outcomes, enhances emergency response capabilities, and enables the provision of better healthcare services to the community.

Community Development and Social Services:

Electricity supports the development of community infrastructure and social services. It enables the establishment of schools, community centers, street lighting, and recreational facilities. Electric-powered water supply systems improve access to clean water, sanitation, and hygiene. These developments contribute to social cohesion, community empowerment, and overall human development.

Increased Connectivity and Market Access: Electricity facilitates better transportation systems, including electric vehicles or charging stations, improving connectivity and mobility options for rural communities. It also supports the establishment of local markets, enables access to e-commerce platforms, and expands market opportunities for rural entrepreneurs by connecting them to regional and global markets.

Social Equity and Gender Empowerment: Rural electrification can help reduce gender disparities and promote social equity. Access to electricity enables women and girls to participate in income-generating activities, educational opportunities, and community decision-making processes. It reduces the burden of household chores and enhances gender equality by providing better access to information, resources, and services.

Overall, rural electrification brings socio-economic transformation by improving living conditions, education, healthcare, agriculture, entrepreneurship, and community development. It empowers communities, enhances opportunities for economic growth, and contributes to sustainable development goals, ultimately bridging the gap between urban and rural areas.

6.2 Electrification and entrepreneurship in rural areas:

Electrification in rural areas can provide significant opportunities for entrepreneurship and economic development. Access to electricity enables the establishment and growth of various businesses and entrepreneurial activities. Here are some ways in which electrification fosters entrepreneurship in rural areas:

Productive Use of Electricity: Reliable electricity access allows rural communities to engage in productive activities that require electricity, such as small-scale manufacturing, agro-processing, and handicraft production. Electric-powered machinery and equipment can enhance productivity, improve product quality, and enable the expansion of businesses. For example, electrification can enable the establishment of grain mills, carpentry workshops, food processing units, and textile production centers.

Chukwujekwu John Okafor and Oko
Obasi

Agricultural Value Addition: Electricity can support agricultural value addition by powering irrigation systems, cold storage facilities, and food processing equipment. Farmers can process and package their produce, increasing its value and enabling access to wider markets. This not only enhances income opportunities for farmers but also creates employment along the agricultural value chain.

Service Sector Development: With access to electricity, rural areas can witness the growth of service-oriented businesses such as repair shops, internet cafes, printing centers, and small-scale hospitality establishments. These businesses cater to the needs of the local community and can also attract tourists and visitors, contributing to the local economy.

Information and Communication Technology (ICT) Services: Electrification enables the establishment of ICT-related businesses, including computer centers, mobile phone repair shops, and internet service providers. These businesses provide essential services and bridge the digital divide in rural areas, allowing individuals and communities to access information, communication, and e-commerce platforms.

Renewable Energy Enterprises: Electrification projects based on renewable energy sources can stimulate entrepreneurship in the renewable energy sector itself. Local entrepreneurs can engage in the installation, operation, and maintenance of renewable energy systems, creating job opportunities and building expertise in clean energy technologies.

Micro-Entrepreneurship and Home-Based Enterprises: Electrification facilitates micro-entrepreneurship and home-based businesses. Rural households can set up small businesses such as tailoring, food processing, handicraft production, and jewelry making that are powered by electricity. These businesses provide additional income streams for households, improve livelihoods, and empower women and marginalized groups to engage in economic activities from the comfort of their homes.

Energy Service Enterprises: With electricity access, energy service enterprises can emerge, providing services such as electrical wiring and installation, appliance repair, solar panel maintenance, and battery charging. These businesses contribute to the local economy and create employment opportunities for trained technicians and electricians.

Chukwujekwu John Okafor and Oko Obasi

Entrepreneurship Training and Support: Alongside electrification initiatives, providing entrepreneurship training, mentorship, and access to financing can help aspiring entrepreneurs in rural areas establish and grow their businesses. Training programs can focus on business management, marketing, financial literacy, and product development. Supportive networks, incubation centers, and access to microfinance institutions can also facilitate the growth of rural entrepreneurship.

It is crucial for electrification programs to consider the specific needs and aspirations of rural communities, engage local stakeholders, and provide an enabling environment for entrepreneurship. By leveraging electricity as a catalyst, rural areas can experience economic growth, job creation, poverty reduction, and improved standards of living.

6.3 Enhancing education and healthcare services: Electrification in rural areas can significantly enhance education and healthcare services, contributing to improved quality of life and sustainable development. Here's how electricity access can positively impact education and healthcare:

Enhancing Education:

1.Lighting and Extended Study Hours: Electricity enables the provision of lighting in schools, allowing for extended study hours and creating a conducive learning environment. Students can study in the evenings and access educational resources, leading to improved academic performance.

2.Audio-Visual Aids and Technology: Electricity enables the use of audio-visual aids, computers, projectors, and internet connectivity in classrooms. This facilitates interactive and engaging teaching methods, improves information dissemination, and enhances digital literacy skills among students.

3.E-Learning and Distance Education: With electricity, rural schools can access e-learning platforms and digital educational resources. It opens up opportunities for distance education programs, online courses, and virtual classrooms, providing access to quality education even in remote areas.

4.ICT-enabled Education: Electricity allows for the integration of Information and Communication Technology (ICT) tools in education. Students can gain digital literacy skills, access online educational content, and participate in online collaboration and communication platforms, expanding their educational horizons.

5.Research and Skill Development: Electricity access supports research activities and skill development programs in schools. Students can conduct science experiments, engage in practical learning, and develop vocational skills using powered equipment and tools.

Enhancing Healthcare:

1.Lighting and Emergency Services: Electricity in healthcare facilities ensures proper lighting for surgeries, examinations, and patient care during night hours. It also enables the use of medical equipment and devices, enhancing the quality of healthcare services. Additionally, electricity enables the operation of refrigeration units for vaccine storage and supports emergency services, such as lighting for ambulances and communication systems.

2.Medical Equipment and Technology: Electricity access allows the use of medical equipment, such as X-ray machines, ultrasound scanners, laboratory analyzers, and electric-powered surgical instruments. This improves diagnostics, treatment, and patient care, reducing the need for patients to travel long distances for specialized healthcare services.

3.Telemedicine and E-Health: With electricity and internet connectivity, rural healthcare facilities can implement telemedicine and e-health initiatives. This enables remote consultations, tele-diagnosis, and access to specialist healthcare services from urban centers, reducing the burden of limited healthcare resources in rural areas.

4.Refrigeration for Medicines and Vaccines: Electricity supports the operation of refrigeration units for proper storage of medicines, vaccines, and blood products. This ensures the availability of essential healthcare supplies and enhances the capacity to respond to healthcare emergencies and epidemics effectively.

5.Maternal and Child Healthcare: Electricity enables the provision of reliable lighting, heating, and cooling in maternity wards and child healthcare facilities. It supports safe childbirth, neonatal care, and the operation of medical equipment for maternal and child health interventions.

6.Health Information Systems: Electricity access allows the implementation of electronic health record systems, data management, and information sharing platforms. This improves healthcare planning, monitoring, and decision-making, leading to better health outcomes in rural areas.

7.Training and Continuing Medical Education: Electricity facilitates training programs and continuing medical education for healthcare professionals in rural areas. With access to electricity, healthcare facilities can conduct training sessions, video conferences, and e-learning programs for skill development and knowledge enhancement.

By integrating electricity into education and healthcare services, rural areas can bridge the gap in access to quality education and healthcare. It empowers individuals, improves health outcomes, and contributes to the overall development of rural communities.

6.4 Improving quality of life and livelihood opportunities: Improving the quality of life and livelihood opportunities is a fundamental goal of rural electrification projects. Access to reliable electricity can have a transformative impact on various aspects of rural communities. Here are some ways in which rural electrification can contribute to improving quality of life and livelihood opportunities:

Enhanced Lighting and Basic Services: Electricity enables access to lighting, which improves safety, security, and productivity. Well-lit homes allow for extended hours of work, study, and social activities. It also facilitates the provision of basic services such as healthcare, education, and communication, which rely on electricity-powered equipment and technologies.

Education and Skill Development: Reliable electricity access supports educational institutions by powering computers, projectors, and other educational tools. It enables e-learning initiatives, access to digital resources, and the use of technology in classrooms. This enhances the educational experience and expands opportunities for skill development, contributing to better livelihood prospects.

Productive Activities and Income Generation: Rural electrification opens up new avenues for income generation and productive activities. It enables the use of electric machinery, equipment, and tools in agriculture, small-scale industries, and entrepreneurship. Electric-powered irrigation systems, grain mills, sewing machines, and refrigeration equipment can increase productivity, reduce manual labor, and improve product quality.

Small Business Development: Access to electricity fosters the growth of small businesses and entrepreneurship in rural areas. It enables the establishment of small shops, cafes, processing units, and other enterprises that require electricity for lighting, refrigeration, machinery, and electronic transactions. These businesses contribute to local employment, economic development, and increased access to goods and services.

Health and Healthcare Services: Electricity plays a vital role in healthcare services and the overall well-being of rural communities. It enables the operation of healthcare facilities, including clinics, hospitals, and medical centers. Electric-powered medical equipment, refrigeration for vaccine storage, lighting for surgeries, and communication systems support improved healthcare delivery and emergency response.

Access to Information and Communication: Electricity facilitates access to information and communication technologies (ICTs) in rural areas. It enables the use of computers, internet connectivity, mobile phones, and telecommunication services. This enhances communication, enables access to e-commerce platforms, empowers individuals with information, and expands social and economic networks.

Community Development and Social Services: Electricity supports the functioning of community centers, schools, libraries, and other social service institutions. It enables the provision of public lighting, community halls for gatherings and events, and access to entertainment and media. These facilities contribute to social cohesion, cultural activities, and the overall development of rural communities.

Improved Health and Well-being: Access to electricity improves health outcomes in rural areas. It enables the use of electric lighting, cooking appliances, and refrigeration for better food preservation. It reduces reliance on traditional and polluting energy sources such as kerosene lamps and biomass stoves, leading to improved indoor air quality and reduced health risks.

Women Empowerment and Gender Equality: Rural electrification can have a significant impact on gender equality and women's empowerment. It reduces the burden of manual labor, especially for women engaged in household chores and income-generating activities. Access to electricity enables women to engage in income-generating activities, education, and community participation, empowering them socially and economically.

Environmental Sustainability: Electrification projects can promote the use of renewable energy sources, contributing to environmental sustainability. By shifting from fossil fuel-based energy sources to clean and renewable options, rural electrification can reduce carbon emissions, mitigate climate change, and protect the natural environment.

To maximize the positive impacts on quality of life and livelihood opportunities, rural electrification projects should be implemented holistically, considering the specific needs, priorities, and aspirations of the local communities. Collaboration with stakeholders, active community engagement, and a focus on inclusive and sustainable development are crucial for ensuring the long-term benefits of electrification.

6.5 Women empowerment and gender-inclusive approaches: Women empowerment and gender-inclusive approaches are essential components of rural electrification projects. By promoting gender equality and empowering women, electrification initiatives can have a more significant and sustainable impact on the social, economic, and environmental aspects of rural communities. Here are some key considerations for promoting women empowerment and gender-inclusive approaches in rural electrification:

Participation and Decision-Making: Ensure the active participation of women in all stages of the electrification project, including planning, design, implementation, and monitoring. Encourage their involvement in decision-making processes and provide opportunities for their voices to be heard. This can be done through community meetings, consultations, and the establishment of inclusive committees or groups.

Capacity Building and Training: Offer training and capacity-building programs specifically targeting women in the community. Provide technical and entrepreneurial skills training to enhance their participation in productive activities and income-generating ventures related to electrification. This includes training in renewable energy technologies, electrical wiring, business management, and financial literacy.

Access to Financing: Facilitate access to financial resources and microfinance opportunities for women entrepreneurs. Support the establishment of women-led businesses in sectors such as energy services, productive use enterprises, and service-oriented activities. Collaboration with local financial institutions and microfinance providers can help create tailored financial products and remove barriers to access for women.

Women-Centric Energy Services: Consider the specific energy needs and priorities of women in rural areas. Address their domestic energy requirements by promoting clean cooking solutions, such as improved cookstoves or biogas systems, which reduce the drudgery of traditional cooking methods and indoor air pollution. Ensure that the electrification project benefits women in their roles as caregivers, homemakers, and income earners.

Livelihood Opportunities: Identify and promote income-generating opportunities for women through the productive use of electricity. Encourage women's participation in activities such as agro-processing, handicraft production, small-scale manufacturing, and service provision, leveraging the availability of reliable electricity. Support the creation of market linkages and value chains that benefit women entrepreneurs.

Gender-Responsive Infrastructure: Ensure that electrification infrastructure takes into account the specific needs and safety concerns of women. This includes the provision of well-lit public spaces, safe access to electricity, and the availability of gender-segregated facilities where necessary, such as separate toilet facilities in public spaces.

Awareness and Sensitization: Conduct awareness campaigns and sensitization programs to promote gender equality, challenge gender norms, and address social barriers that hinder women's participation in electrification activities. Engage with community leaders, religious institutions, and local organizations to foster a supportive environment for women's empowerment and challenge gender stereotypes.

Data Collection and Monitoring: Collect gender-disaggregated data to monitor the impact of electrification projects on women's empowerment and well-being. This data can help identify specific challenges, gaps, and opportunities for further intervention. Regular monitoring and evaluation should include gender-sensitive indicators to assess the project's gender equality outcomes.

Collaboration and Partnerships: Foster partnerships with local women's organizations, NGOs, and government agencies to leverage their expertise and promote gender equality in electrification initiatives. Collaborate with existing women's networks and platforms to ensure their representation and active engagement in project activities.

Policy and Institutional Support: Advocate for gender-responsive policies and regulations in the energy sector. Engage with government agencies and policymakers to promote gender mainstreaming in electrification programs and ensure that gender considerations are integrated into the broader energy policy framework.

Promoting women empowerment and gender inclusion in rural electrification projects not only advances social equity but also enhances the effectiveness, sustainability, and long-term impact of electrification initiatives. It empowers women to become agents of change, promotes economic growth, and contributes to the overall development of rural communities.

6.6 Environmental sustainability and clean energy adoption: Environmental sustainability and clean energy adoption are crucial considerations in rural electrification projects. Here are some key aspects related to environmental sustainability and clean energy adoption:

Renewable Energy Sources: Promote the use of renewable energy sources such as solar, wind, hydro, and biomass for rural electrification. These sources are clean, abundant, and sustainable, reducing dependence on fossil fuels and minimizing greenhouse gas emissions.

Off-Grid and Mini-Grid Solutions: In areas where grid extension is not feasible or cost-effective, consider off-grid and mini-grid solutions powered by renewable energy. These decentralized systems provide reliable electricity access while minimizing transmission losses and reducing environmental impact.

Energy Efficiency and Demand-Side Management: Encourage energy efficiency practices and demand-side management to optimize energy use. Promote energy-efficient appliances, lighting solutions, and productive equipment. Implement awareness programs to educate communities on the importance of energy conservation.

Sustainable Infrastructure Design: Incorporate sustainable design principles into the infrastructure planning and implementation process. This includes using eco-friendly construction materials, optimizing building designs for energy efficiency, and considering the environmental impact of transmission and distribution infrastructure.

Chukwujekwu John Okafor and Oko Obasi

Environmental Impact Assessment: Conduct comprehensive environmental impact assessments to identify and mitigate potential negative environmental effects of the electrification project. Assess the impacts on biodiversity, ecosystems, water resources, and local communities. Implement measures to minimize and mitigate adverse effects during construction and operation.

Waste Management and Pollution Control: Develop waste management protocols to handle and dispose of electronic waste and other hazardous materials generated from the electrification project. Implement pollution control measures to minimize air and water pollution associated with energy generation, storage, and distribution.

Reforestation and Afforestation: Encourage reforestation and afforestation initiatives as part of the electrification project. Planting trees helps sequester carbon dioxide, enhance biodiversity, and contribute to ecosystem restoration. Engage local communities in tree planting activities and promote sustainable land management practices.

Clean Cooking Solutions: Address the issue of indoor air pollution by promoting clean cooking solutions. Encourage the use of efficient cookstoves powered by clean fuels or renewable energy sources. This reduces reliance on traditional biomass fuels and improves indoor air quality, particularly for households in rural areas.

Community Engagement and Education: Engage the local community in environmental awareness and education programs. Raise awareness about the benefits of clean energy, sustainable practices, and the importance of environmental conservation. Empower communities to actively participate in decision-making processes related to the electrification project.

Monitoring and Reporting: Establish mechanisms for monitoring and reporting the environmental performance of the electrification project. Regularly assess and evaluate the project's environmental impact and progress towards sustainability goals. Share the results transparently with stakeholders and incorporate feedback for continuous improvement.

Collaboration with environmental experts, partnerships with renewable energy companies, and adherence to relevant environmental regulations and standards are vital for ensuring the successful integration of environmental sustainability and clean energy adoption in rural electrification projects.

Chukwujekwu John Okafor and Oko
Obasi

CHAPTER 7

POLICY, REGULATION, AND INSTITUTIONAL FRAMEWORK

7.1 National and regional policies for rural electrification: National and regional policies for rural electrification vary across countries and regions depending on their specific needs, resources, and development goals. However, several common approaches and strategies are often employed to promote rural electrification. Here are some examples:

National Electrification Plans: Many countries develop comprehensive national electrification plans that include specific targets and strategies for rural electrification. These plans outline the government's commitment to extending electricity access to rural areas and provide a roadmap for achieving this goal.

Financial Incentives and Subsidies: Governments

often provide financial incentives and subsidies to encourage investment in rural electrification projects. These incentives may include tax breaks, grants, low-interest loans, or subsidies for the cost of infrastructure installation and operation.

Public-Private Partnerships (PPPs): Governments collaborate with private companies and organizations through PPPs to leverage expertise and resources for rural electrification. These partnerships can help attract investment, improve project management, and promote sustainable and efficient service delivery.

Off-grid and Renewable Energy Solutions: In areas where extending the central power grid is challenging or economically unfeasible, governments promote the use of off-grid and decentralized renewable energy solutions. This includes solar home systems, mini-grids, and small-scale hydro or wind power projects. Policies may focus on facilitating the installation, operation, and maintenance of such systems.

Regulatory Reforms: Governments may enact regulatory reforms to create an enabling environment for rural electrification. This includes streamlining procedures, reducing bureaucratic hurdles, and establishing clear guidelines for private sector participation in the electricity sector.

Regulatory frameworks often aim to promote competition, ensure affordable tariffs, and protect the rights of consumers.

Capacity Building and Training: Policies for rural electrification often include initiatives to enhance the skills and knowledge of local communities, technicians, and entrepreneurs. Training programs may cover aspects such as renewable energy technologies, operation and maintenance of electrification systems, and entrepreneurship in the energy sector.

Community Participation and Ownership: Encouraging community participation and ownership in rural electrification projects can enhance sustainability and ensure the systems meet local needs. Policies may emphasize community engagement, cooperative models, and local governance structures to foster a sense of ownership and responsibility.

Data Collection and Monitoring: Governments establish mechanisms to collect data on electricity access and monitor progress in rural electrification. This enables evidence-based decision-making, helps identify areas with the greatest needs, and allows for the evaluation of policy effectiveness.

It is important to note that the specific policies and

approaches can vary significantly depending on the country and region. Each government tailors its strategies to suit local conditions, resources, and priorities.

7.2 Regulatory frameworks and legal considerations:

Regulatory frameworks and legal considerations play a crucial role in facilitating rural electrification and ensuring the effective and sustainable delivery of electricity services. Here are some key elements and considerations related to regulatory frameworks:

Licensing and Permits: Regulatory frameworks establish licensing procedures and permit requirements for electricity service providers, including those operating in rural areas. These processes ensure that service providers meet certain technical, financial, and operational criteria to ensure safe and reliable electricity supply.

Tariff Regulation: Regulators oversee the pricing of electricity services to ensure they are fair, affordable, and reflect the cost of supply. Tariff regulation may involve setting tariffs for different customer categories, approving tariff methodologies, and monitoring compliance with pricing regulations.

Market Structure and Competition: Regulatory frameworks define the market structure for electricity services, including whether it is a vertically integrated monopoly, a competitive market, or a combination of both. Regulators may promote competition through unbundling of generation, transmission, and distribution functions, and establishing rules for fair market access.

Quality of Service Standards: Regulators establish and enforce quality of service standards to ensure that electricity service providers deliver reliable and adequate power supply. These standards may include parameters such as voltage levels, frequency, outage durations, and customer service requirements.

7.2.5 Consumer Protection: Regulatory frameworks often incorporate provisions to protect consumer rights and ensure fair treatment. This may include measures such as transparent billing practices, dispute resolution mechanisms, and safeguards against anti-competitive behavior.

7.2.6 Environmental and Social Impact Assessment: Governments require environmental and social impact assessments to evaluate the potential effects of rural electrification projects on the environment, local communities, and cultural heritage. These assessments help identify mitigation measures and ensure compliance with environmental and social standards.

7.2.7 Grid Interconnection and Access: Regulations define the rules and procedures for grid interconnection, enabling rural electrification projects to connect to the national or regional power grid. Access to the grid ensures reliable power supply and facilitates the integration of renewable energy sources.

7.2.8 Monitoring and Compliance: Regulatory frameworks include provisions for monitoring and enforcing compliance with regulations and standards. Regulators oversee the performance of electricity service providers, conduct audits, and impose penalties for non-compliance.

7.2.9 Policy Stability and Long-term Planning: Governments strive to provide policy stability and long-term planning frameworks to attract investment in rural electrification. Predictable policies and regulations create a favorable environment for private sector participation and ensure continuity of electrification efforts.

It is important for regulatory frameworks to strike a balance between ensuring a supportive environment for private sector investment and safeguarding the interests of consumers and the public. The specific regulatory provisions and legal considerations may differ from country to country, reflecting the unique energy landscape, institutional setup, and development priorities of each jurisdiction.

7.3 Institutional capacity building and governance structures: Institutional capacity building and governance structures are essential for the effective implementation and management of rural electrification initiatives. They help ensure efficient decision-making, coordination, and oversight of the electrification process. Here are some key elements related to institutional capacity building and governance structures:

Energy Planning and Coordination: Establishing dedicated institutions or departments responsible for energy planning and coordination is crucial. These entities can develop national or regional energy plans, set electrification targets, coordinate activities among various stakeholders, and provide overall direction to the electrification efforts.

Regulatory Bodies: Independent regulatory bodies or agencies play a vital role in overseeing the electricity sector, including rural electrification. These entities ensure compliance with regulations, monitor service quality, approve tariffs, promote competition, and protect the interests of consumers. They require skilled staff with expertise in energy regulation and governance.

Institutional Collaboration: Effective rural electrification requires collaboration among various institutions and stakeholders, including government agencies, utilities, private sector entities, community organizations, and development partners. Institutional frameworks should facilitate collaboration, information sharing, and coordination to leverage resources, expertise, and experiences.

Capacity Development Programs: Training and capacity development programs are necessary to enhance the skills and knowledge of personnel involved in rural electrification projects. These programs can cover technical aspects of electrification, project management, policy development, regulatory frameworks, financial management, and community engagement.

Decentralized Decision-making: In decentralized governance structures, decision-making authority is devolved to local or regional levels. This allows for more tailored and context-specific approaches to rural electrification, considering the unique needs, resources, and priorities of different areas. Local governance structures can actively involve communities in decision-making processes and ensure their participation in electrification initiatives.

Project Management Units: Establishing dedicated project management units (PMUs) can streamline the implementation and monitoring of rural electrification projects. PMUs are responsible for project planning, procurement, contract management, construction supervision, and overall project coordination. They ensure timely execution and adherence to quality standards.

Monitoring and Evaluation: Robust monitoring and evaluation mechanisms are essential to track the progress, performance, and impact of rural electrification projects. This includes collecting data on electricity access, service quality, financial sustainability, and socio-economic benefits. Effective monitoring and evaluation help identify challenges, inform policy adjustments, and support evidence-based decision-making.

Public Awareness and Stakeholder Engagement: Effective governance structures promote public awareness and stakeholder engagement throughout the electrification process. This includes conducting public consultations, raising awareness about the benefits of electricity access, and involving communities in project design, implementation, and monitoring. Active engagement fosters ownership, increases project acceptance, and helps address community concerns.

Financial Management and Accountability: Robust financial management practices and accountability mechanisms are essential to ensure transparent and efficient use of resources. Strong financial management systems, including budgeting, auditing, and reporting, help track expenditure, prevent corruption, and build trust among stakeholders.

Knowledge Sharing and Collaboration: Institutions involved in rural electrification should facilitate knowledge sharing, exchange of best practices, and collaboration with regional and international partners. This can help leverage experiences, access technical expertise, and stay updated on technological advancements, policy innovations, and funding opportunities.

Institutional capacity building and effective governance structures create an enabling environment for rural electrification, enhancing the efficiency, sustainability, and impact of electrification efforts.

7.4 Public-private partnerships and stakeholder

collaboration: Public-private partnerships (PPPs) and stakeholder collaboration are two approaches aimed at fostering cooperation between different entities to achieve common goals and address societal challenges. While they are distinct concepts, they often go hand in hand, as effective stakeholder collaboration is crucial for the success of PPPs.

Public-private partnerships involve the collaboration between public sector entities (such as government agencies or local authorities) and private sector organizations (such as companies or non-profit organizations). These partnerships leverage the respective strengths of both sectors to jointly deliver services, infrastructure projects, or address social issues.

Stakeholder collaboration, on the other hand, emphasizes the involvement and cooperation of various stakeholders who have an interest or are affected by a particular project or initiative. These stakeholders can include government agencies, private sector entities, civil society organizations, local communities, and individuals.

The benefits of public-private partnerships and stakeholder collaboration include:

1.Resource sharing and efficiency: PPPs allow for the pooling of financial, technical, and human resources from both the public and private sectors, leading to more efficient and effective outcomes. Stakeholder collaboration ensures that diverse perspectives and expertise are taken into account, leading to better-informed decisions and solutions.

2.Innovation and expertise: Private sector involvement in PPPs brings in innovation, entrepreneurial spirit, and specialized expertise, which can enhance the quality and efficiency of projects. Stakeholder collaboration enables the integration of different knowledge domains and experiences, fostering innovative approaches and solutions.

3.Risk sharing: In PPPs, risks and responsibilities are shared between public and private partners. This can provide a more balanced and sustainable risk management framework. Stakeholder collaboration allows for risk identification, assessment, and mitigation strategies to be developed collectively, reducing the potential negative impacts on all parties involved.

4.Accountability and transparency: PPPs and stakeholder collaboration promote accountability through clear roles, responsibilities, and performance metrics. Engaging stakeholders in decision-making processes ensures transparency and enhances public trust by providing opportunities for public input and scrutiny.

5.Social impact and sustainability: By combining

the resources and expertise of both sectors and engaging stakeholders, PPPs can address social challenges more comprehensively. Stakeholder collaboration facilitates a holistic approach to problem-solving, taking into account social, environmental, and economic aspects, thereby promoting long-term sustainability.

Successful implementation of PPPs and stakeholder collaboration requires effective communication, trust-building, and alignment of interests among the involved parties. It is essential to establish clear objectives, governance structures, and mechanisms for ongoing dialogue and collaboration. Additionally, legal frameworks, regulatory environments, and financial models need to support and incentivize such partnerships and collaborations.

7.5 Financing mechanisms and incentives for rural electrification: Financing mechanisms and incentives play a crucial role in mobilizing the necessary funds and attracting investment for rural electrification. They help overcome financial barriers, reduce risks, and create favorable conditions for project development. Here are some common financing mechanisms and incentives for rural electrification:

Government Budget Allocation: Governments

allocate funds from their national budgets to support rural electrification initiatives. These funds can be used for infrastructure development, capacity building, community engagement, and project implementation. Budgetary allocations demonstrate government commitment and provide a stable and predictable source of financing.

Subsidies and Grants: Subsidies and grants are provided to reduce the financial burden on rural electrification projects. They can be directed towards infrastructure investment, technology deployment, or operational costs. Subsidies can target both supply-side (e.g., developers, utilities) and demand-side (e.g., end-users) to promote affordability and accessibility.

Soft Loans and Credit Facilities: Governments, development banks, and financial institutions offer soft loans and credit facilities with favorable terms and conditions to promote rural electrification. These loans often have low-interest rates, extended repayment periods, and flexible collateral requirements, reducing the financial burden on project developers and facilitating access to financing.

Public-Private Partnerships (PPPs): PPPs leverage private sector expertise and resources for rural electrification projects. Governments provide incentives such as tax breaks, land access, or guarantees to attract private investment. PPPs can be structured in various forms, including Build-Operate-Transfer (BOT), Build-Own-Operate (BOO), or joint ventures, depending on the specific project and regulatory framework.

Microfinance and Community-Based Financing: Microfinance institutions (MFIs) provide small-scale loans and financial services to rural communities and entrepreneurs for electrification projects. Community-based financing models, such as revolving funds or cooperatives, pool resources from community members to fund electrification initiatives. These mechanisms promote local ownership and empower communities to take part in the electrification process.

Carbon Financing and Climate Funds: Projects that utilize renewable energy sources for rural electrification can access climate funds and carbon financing mechanisms. These funds, such as the Clean Development Mechanism (CDM), Green Climate Fund (GCF), or carbon credits, provide additional revenue streams that support project viability and financial sustainability.

Result-Based Financing: Result-based financing mechanisms incentivize project developers based on the achievement of pre-defined performance targets. Payments are made upon the successful delivery of electricity services, such as the number of connections, energy generation, or improved energy efficiency. These mechanisms align incentives with project outcomes and promote accountability.

Crowdfunding and Innovative Financing: Crowdfunding platforms and innovative financing mechanisms, such as social impact bonds or energy cooperatives, allow individuals and organizations to contribute funds directly to rural electrification projects. These mechanisms tap into the power of the crowd and provide an alternative source of financing beyond traditional channels.

Tax Incentives and Customs Duty Exemptions: Governments can provide tax incentives, including tax holidays or exemptions, to attract private investment in rural electrification. Customs duty exemptions on equipment, machinery, and renewable energy technologies can reduce project costs and make investments more financially viable.

Feed-in Tariffs and Power Purchase Agreements: Feed-in tariffs (FiTs) and power purchase agreements (PPAs) provide guaranteed payments for electricity generated from renewable energy sources. These mechanisms ensure a stable revenue stream for project developers and incentivize investments in rural electrification projects using renewable energy technologies.

It is important to note that the availability and suitability of financing mechanisms and incentives may vary depending on the country's specific context, policy environment, and financial sector development. Governments often adopt a combination of these mechanisms, tailored to local conditions, to attract the necessary funding for rural electrification.

CHAPTER 8

CASE STUDIES AND BEST PRACTICES

8.1 In-depth analysis of successful rural electrification projects:

Successful rural electrification projects can have a transformative impact on the lives of people living in rural areas. Access to electricity can bring numerous benefits, including improved education, healthcare, economic development, and overall quality of life. In this in-depth analysis, we will explore the key factors that contribute to the success of rural electrification projects.

Planning and Policy: Successful projects start with a clear and well-defined plan. Governments and stakeholders need to establish policies and regulations that support rural electrification, including financial incentives, technical standards, and legal frameworks. Effective coordination between government agencies, utilities, and local communities is crucial for the success of the project.

Appropriate Technology: Choosing the right

technology for rural electrification is vital. It should be suitable for the local context, taking into account factors like energy demand, resource availability, and infrastructure limitations. Renewable energy sources such as solar, wind, and mini-hydro can be cost-effective and environmentally friendly options for rural areas. Decentralized systems like microgrids can also be effective in reaching remote communities.

Community Engagement: Active community participation and engagement are essential for the sustainability and success of electrification projects. Local communities should be involved in the planning, implementation, and decision-making processes. Understanding the specific needs and priorities of the community helps in designing a system that addresses their requirements. Community ownership models, such as cooperatives, can foster a sense of responsibility and ensure long-term sustainability.

Financing and Funding: Adequate financing is crucial for the implementation of rural electrification projects. Governments, development agencies, and private sector investments can provide the necessary funds. Innovative financing mechanisms, such as public-private partnerships, grants, microfinance, and crowd-funding, can be explored to ensure affordability for both the project and the end-users. Long-term financial sustainability should be considered, including revenue collection mechanisms and cost recovery strategies.

Infrastructure Development: Rural electrification requires the development of robust and reliable infrastructure. This includes power generation facilities, transmission and distribution networks, and last-mile connectivity. The infrastructure should be designed to withstand the local environmental conditions and be scalable to meet future needs. Embracing smart grid technologies and efficient energy storage solutions can optimize energy management and improve the reliability of the system.

Capacity Building and Skill Development: Building local capacity and empowering communities are critical for the long-term success of electrification projects. Training programs should be provided to local technicians, entrepreneurs, and community members to enhance their technical skills, operation, and maintenance capabilities. This enables them to take ownership of the system, carry out basic repairs, and ensure its sustainability.

Monitoring and Evaluation: Regular monitoring and evaluation help identify challenges, measure progress, and make necessary adjustments. Key performance indicators should be established to assess the impact of electrification on various sectors such as education, healthcare, agriculture, and small-scale industries. Feedback from the community should be incorporated into decision-making processes to ensure the project's effectiveness.

Post-Electrification Support: Successful projects go beyond the initial electrification phase. Ongoing support is essential to maximize the benefits of access to electricity. This can include programs for income-generating activities, entrepreneurship, and access to modern appliances. Additionally, maintenance and repair services, as well as reliable customer support, should be available to address any operational issues.

8.2 Case studies of successful rural electrification projects: There have been several successful rural electrification projects implemented worldwide. Here are seven case studies of notable projects:

1.The National Rural Electrification Program (NREP) in India: India's NREP was launched in 2005 with the aim of providing electricity access to all rural households in the country. The program has been highly successful, with millions of households gaining access to electricity through grid extension, renewable energy mini-grids, and solar home systems. The NREP has played a crucial role in improving the quality of life, fostering economic development, and promoting social inclusion in rural India.

2.The Luz y Fuerza del Centro (LyFC) program in Mexico: LyFC, a public utility company in Mexico, implemented a rural electrification program targeting remote and marginalized communities. The initiative involved the installation of solar-powered microgrids and the provision of affordable electricity to underserved areas. The LyFC program has significantly improved access to clean energy, enabling communities to engage in income-generating activities, enhance education and healthcare services, and improve overall living conditions.

3.Bangladesh Rural Electrification Project: The Solar Energy Foundation (SEF)in Bangladesh has implemented a successful rural electrification project using solar home systems (SHS). The initiative aimed to provide off-grid communities with affordable and reliable electricity. By distributing SHS to households, the SEF has empowered rural communities, allowing them to run businesses, extend working hours, and access information through appliances and communication devices. The Bangladesh Rural Electrification Board (BREB) also implemented a successful rural electrification initiative, known as the "Palli Bidyut" program. The project aimed to provide electricity to remote villages using decentralized renewable energy sources, including solar, wind, and biogas. The BREB collaborated with local communities, NGOs, and international organizations to establish power distribution networks. These projects have played a pivotal role in reducing energy poverty in rural Bangladesh

.

4.The Zanzibar Renewable Energy Development Program (ZREDP) in Tanzania:

The ZREDP, implemented in Zanzibar, Tanzania, focused on electrifying remote islands using renewable energy sources. The project utilized a combination of solar PV systems, wind turbines, and battery storage to establish microgrids. The ZREDP has transformed the lives of island communities, enabling access to electricity for households, schools, health clinics, and businesses. It has contributed to socioeconomic development, improved education and healthcare outcomes, and reduced reliance on expensive and polluting diesel generators.

5.The Lao Rural Electrification Project (LREP) in

Laos: The LREP aimed to expand electricity access to rural areas of Laos, where communities had limited or no access to electricity. The project combined grid extension, standalone solar PV systems, and small hydro schemes to electrify remote villages. The LREP has positively impacted rural livelihoods by providing power for lighting, productive use activities, and the operation of community services. It has improved education, healthcare, and communication services, fostering economic growth and social well-being.

6.Solar Electrification Project in Morocco: In Morocco, the government implemented the "Moroccan Solar Plan" to bring electricity to remote rural areas. The project involved the installation of solar photovoltaic systems in off-grid villages. The government partnered with local communities and international organizations to provide affordable and sustainable electricity. As a result, thousands of rural households gained access to electricity, improving their quality of life, education, and healthcare

7.Electrification of Villages in Peru: The Peruvian government implemented the National Rural Electrification Program (Programa Nacional de Electrificación Rural - PRONER) to bring electricity to remote areas of the country. The project utilized a combination of renewable energy sources, such as solar, wind, and hydropower, to electrify rural communities. The initiative involved the installation of microgrids and the training of local technicians to maintain and operate the systems. This project has positively impacted the lives of rural Peruvians, enabling access to modern amenities and fostering economic development.

These case studies highlight successful rural electrification projects that have made significant strides in improving the lives of rural communities by providing them with access to clean and affordable energy.

8.2   Lessons learned from different regions and contexts:

Lessons learned from different regions and contexts can provide valuable insights and knowledge that can be applied in various situations. Here are some examples:

Community Engagement and Empowerment: In regions with strong community engagement and empowerment initiatives, such as certain parts of Scandinavia, communities have shown higher levels of social cohesion, trust, and resilience. This approach highlights the importance of involving local communities in decision-making processes and fostering a sense of ownership and responsibility.

Sustainable Development: Countries like Costa Rica and Bhutan have prioritized sustainable development and environmental conservation. Lessons from these regions include the importance of environmental stewardship, the promotion of renewable energy sources, and the integration of sustainability principles into economic planning and policies.

Disaster Preparedness and Resilience: Areas prone to natural disasters, like Japan, have developed robust disaster preparedness measures. These regions emphasize early warning systems, infrastructure resilience, community education, and disaster response coordination. Lessons include the significance of investing in disaster risk reduction, preparedness training, and effective communication during emergencies.

Education Reform: Countries such as Finland and Singapore have implemented successful education reforms. These regions focus on teacher training, equitable access to education, student-centered learning, and holistic assessment methods. Lessons include the importance of high-quality teacher education, flexible teaching methodologies, and a balanced emphasis on academic and non-academic skills.

Healthcare Delivery: Regions with efficient healthcare systems, like Germany and the Netherlands, have implemented universal healthcare coverage, emphasis on preventive care, and strong primary care networks. Lessons include the value of comprehensive health insurance, strong primary care infrastructure, and proactive public health strategies.

Conflict Resolution and Peacebuilding: Post-conflict regions, like Rwanda, have made significant progress in reconciliation and peacebuilding. Lessons include the importance of truth and reconciliation processes, community-based initiatives, intergroup dialogue, and efforts to address the root causes of conflict.

Urban Planning and Transportation: Cities like Copenhagen, Denmark, and Curitiba, Brazil, have prioritized sustainable urban planning and transportation systems. Lessons include the promotion of cycling and walking infrastructure, efficient public transportation, mixed-use zoning, and green spaces, leading to reduced congestion, pollution, and improved quality of life.

These are just a few examples of lessons learned from different regions and contexts. Each region offers unique insights and experiences that can inform decision-making and contribute to positive outcomes in various domains.

8.3 Replication and scalability of successful models:

The replication and scalability of successful rural electrification models are crucial for achieving widespread access to electricity in rural areas. Here are key considerations for replicating and scaling up successful models:

Adaptability: Successful models need to be adaptable to different geographic, social, and economic contexts. What works in one region may not be directly applicable to another. Replication requires a thorough understanding of the local conditions, including energy demand, resource availability, infrastructure constraints, and cultural factors. Flexibility in design and implementation is essential to tailor the model to each specific context.

Knowledge Sharing and Collaboration: Sharing knowledge and best practices among stakeholders is vital for successful replication. Governments, development agencies, non-profit organizations, and private sector entities should collaborate and exchange experiences to learn from each other's successes and challenges. Establishing platforms for knowledge sharing, such as conferences, workshops, and online networks, facilitates the dissemination of information and promotes collaboration.

Policy and Regulatory Support: Favorable policies and regulations play a crucial role in replication and scalability. Governments should create an enabling environment by developing supportive policies, regulatory frameworks, and financial incentives. Clear guidelines for project implementation, standardization of procedures, and streamlined approval processes can facilitate replication. Policy consistency and long-term commitment are necessary to attract investments and ensure the sustainability of electrification efforts.

Investment and Financing: Access to adequate investment and financing mechanisms is essential for replication and scalability. Governments can allocate funds or provide subsidies to replicate successful models. Development finance institutions and impact investors can play a crucial role in mobilizing capital for rural electrification projects. Innovative financing approaches, such as blended finance models and public-private partnerships, can leverage resources and attract private sector participation.

Capacity Building: Building local capacity is vital for

replication and scalability. Training programs should be implemented to enhance the technical skills of local technicians, entrepreneurs, and community members. This includes training in system installation, operation, and maintenance, as well as entrepreneurship and business management skills. Building a pool of skilled professionals and empowering local communities helps ensure the sustainability and long-term success of replicated projects.

Public Awareness and Participation: Generating public awareness and participation is essential for the replication of successful models. Outreach programs, community engagement activities, and awareness campaigns should be conducted to educate rural communities about the benefits of electrification and their role in the process. Engaging local communities from the outset builds a sense of ownership and facilitates the adoption and acceptance of the replicated models.

Scalability Planning: Replicating successful models requires careful scalability planning. The replication process should be phased, starting with pilot projects to test feasibility and address challenges. Scalability plans should consider the capacity of local institutions, the availability of resources, and the scalability of infrastructure. Assessing potential barriers and developing strategies to overcome them ensures a smooth and efficient scaling process.

Monitoring and Evaluation: Continuous monitoring and evaluation are essential during the replication and scaling process. Regular assessments help identify bottlenecks, measure progress, and make necessary adjustments. Monitoring indicators should be established to assess the impact and effectiveness of replicated projects. Feedback from stakeholders and end-users should be incorporated into the replication process to ensure continuous improvement.

By considering these factors, successful rural electrification models can be replicated and scaled up effectively, bringing electricity access to a larger number of rural communities and contributing to sustainable development.

CHAPTER 9

FUTURE TRENDS AND CHALLENGES

9.1   Emerging technologies and their potential in rural electrification:

Emerging technologies have the potential to revolutionize rural electrification efforts by offering innovative solutions that are cost-effective, environmentally friendly, and tailored to the specific needs of rural communities. Here are some key emerging technologies and their potential in rural electrification:

Decentralized Renewable Energy Systems: Decentralized renewable energy systems, such as solar panels, small wind turbines, and mini-hydro power plants, have gained significant attention in rural electrification. These systems can be deployed on a small scale, making them suitable for remote areas. They provide clean and reliable power, reducing dependence on centralized grid infrastructure. Advanced technologies in solar panels, such as thin-film solar cells and solar trackers, enhance energy efficiency and increase energy production.

Energy Storage Technologies: Energy storage technologies, including advanced batteries and innovative solutions like pumped hydro storage and compressed air energy storage, can play a crucial role in rural electrification. These technologies enable the storage of excess energy generated during favorable conditions for use during periods of low generation or high demand. Energy storage enhances the reliability and stability of decentralized systems and allows for a more efficient utilization of renewable energy resources.

Smart Grid Solutions: Smart grid technologies can optimize the management of rural electrification systems. Advanced monitoring and control systems, along with sensors and communication networks, enable real-time data collection, load management, and energy optimization. Smart grids enhance grid reliability, facilitate efficient demand-response mechanisms, and support the integration of renewable energy sources. They also enable remote monitoring and maintenance of electrification systems, reducing downtime and operational costs.

Internet of Things (IoT) and Connectivity: IoT technologies and connectivity solutions can enhance rural electrification by enabling remote monitoring, data collection, and control of energy systems. IoT devices, such as smart meters and energy management systems, can provide real-time information on energy consumption, enabling efficient energy planning and billing. Connectivity options like satellite-based internet and wireless networks bridge the digital divide, facilitating access to information, e-commerce, and telecommunication services in rural areas.

Mini-Grids and Microgrids: Mini-grids and microgrids are localized electricity distribution systems that can serve clusters of households or communities. These systems can be powered by renewable energy sources and are particularly suitable for rural areas with limited access to the main grid. Advanced control and management technologies optimize power distribution, load balancing, and grid stability in mini-grid and microgrid setups. These solutions enable localized energy generation, consumption, and trading within the community, fostering economic development and energy independence.

Pay-as-You-Go (PAYG) Systems: PAYG systems leverage mobile payment technologies to enable affordable access to electricity for rural communities. These systems allow users to pay for electricity in small increments as they use it, often through mobile phone-based platforms. PAYG systems, combined with decentralized renewable energy solutions, provide affordable and scalable options for rural electrification, particularly in regions with limited access to banking and traditional financing mechanisms.

Energy-Efficient Appliances and Productive Use: Promoting the use of energy-efficient appliances and productive end-use applications is crucial for maximizing the impact of rural electrification. Energy-efficient appliances reduce energy consumption and enhance the affordability of electricity for rural households. Additionally, supporting productive end-use applications, such as small-scale agricultural processing, cottage industries, and community services, can create income-generating opportunities and contribute to the economic development of rural areas.

These emerging technologies hold great promise for accelerating rural electrification efforts worldwide. However, successful implementation requires careful consideration of local conditions, affordability, capacity building, and long-term sustainability. Collaboration between governments, development agencies, private sector entities, and local communities is essential for leveraging these technologies effectively in rural electrification projects.

9.2 Climate change and resilient electrification solutions: Climate change and the transition to resilient electrification solutions are critical in mitigating the impacts of global warming and achieving a sustainable future. Here are some key considerations and solutions:

Renewable Energy Transition: Shifting from fossil fuel-based energy sources to renewable energy is crucial. Expanding the deployment of solar, wind, hydro, geothermal, and tidal energy can significantly reduce greenhouse gas emissions. This transition requires supportive policies, incentives, and investments in renewable energy infrastructure.

Energy Storage: Implementing effective energy storage solutions is essential for resilient electrification. Batteries, pumped hydro storage, compressed air energy storage, and other emerging technologies help store renewable energy for times of high demand or low generation. Energy storage systems improve grid reliability, enhance resilience, and enable the integration of intermittent renewable energy sources.

Smart Grids and Microgrids: Developing smart grid systems that optimize energy generation, distribution, and consumption can enhance efficiency and resilience. Microgrids, which are localized, self-contained energy systems, can operate independently or in connection with the main grid, enabling communities to maintain power during outages and emergencies.

Electrification of Transportation: Transitioning from fossil fuel-powered vehicles to electric vehicles (EVs) significantly reduces emissions. Promoting EV adoption through incentives, charging infrastructure expansion, and collaboration with the private sector can accelerate this transition. Electrifying public transportation and freight systems further contribute to emissions reduction.

Energy Efficiency and Demand-Side Management: Energy efficiency measures play a crucial role in resilient electrification. Retrofitting buildings with energy-efficient technologies, implementing efficient lighting systems, and adopting smart appliances can reduce energy consumption. Demand-side management strategies, such as time-of-use pricing and demand response programs, help balance energy supply and demand while reducing stress on the grid.

Decentralized Energy Generation: Distributed energy generation through rooftop solar panels, small-scale wind turbines, and community-owned renewable energy projects enhances grid resilience. By diversifying energy sources and reducing transmission losses, decentralized generation can improve reliability and provide localized power during disruptions.

Climate Resilience Planning: Resilient electrification solutions should consider climate change impacts. This includes designing infrastructure to withstand extreme weather events, such as storms or floods, and assessing vulnerabilities and adaptation strategies for energy systems in vulnerable areas.

International Cooperation: Addressing climate change and resilient electrification requires global collaboration. Sharing best practices, technology transfer, and financial support for developing countries can help accelerate the transition to sustainable energy systems worldwide.

It is crucial to integrate these solutions into comprehensive energy plans, backed by supportive policies, regulatory frameworks, and public awareness campaigns. By embracing resilient electrification, we can reduce greenhouse gas emissions, increase energy access, and build a more sustainable and climate-resilient future.

9.3   Addressing energy poverty and access gaps: Addressing energy poverty and access gaps is a crucial global challenge. Here are some innovative approaches and technological advancements that can help bridge these gaps:

Off-grid Renewable Energy Solutions: Off-grid renewable energy systems, such as solar home systems and mini-grids, provide decentralized power generation to communities without access to the main power grid. These systems are cost-effective, environmentally friendly, and can provide electricity for lighting, cooking, and powering essential appliances.

Pay-as-you-go (PAYG) Systems: PAYG models allow users to access energy services by paying in small increments, typically through mobile payments. This approach makes energy solutions more affordable and accessible to individuals with limited financial resources, as they can pay for energy services in a way that aligns with their income patterns.

Energy Storage Technologies: Energy storage technologies, such as advanced batteries, are critical for addressing energy access gaps. They enable the efficient use and distribution of electricity generated from intermittent renewable energy sources, ensuring a reliable and continuous power supply.

Microfinance and Energy Financing: Innovative financing mechanisms, including microfinance and energy financing, can help overcome the financial barriers that hinder energy access for marginalized communities. These approaches provide affordable loans and flexible payment options, making clean energy solutions more attainable.

Mobile Technology and Digital Platforms: Mobile technology and digital platforms can play a significant role in improving energy access. They can be used for payment systems, energy monitoring, and data collection, enabling better management of energy resources and facilitating the provision of energy services in remote areas.

Community Engagement and Capacity Building: Engaging local communities and building their capacity is vital for sustainable energy access.

Community-led initiatives, training programs, and awareness campaigns can empower individuals to take ownership of energy projects, ensuring their long-term success and impact.

Policy and Regulatory Support: Governments play a crucial role in addressing energy poverty and access gaps by creating supportive policies and regulations. This includes promoting renewable energy investments, incentivizing private sector participation, and establishing frameworks for decentralized energy solutions.

International Partnerships and Funding: International collaborations and funding mechanisms can accelerate progress in addressing energy poverty. Partnerships between governments, organizations, and stakeholders can leverage expertise, resources, and funding to scale up energy access initiatives globally.

Energy-Efficient Solutions: Promoting energy-efficient technologies and practices is essential to maximize the impact of available energy resources. Energy-efficient appliances, building designs, and productive end-use applications can help optimize energy consumption and reduce overall energy demand.

Innovative Business Models: The development of

innovative business models can drive sustainable energy access. Social enterprises, public-private partnerships, and community-driven models can create viable and scalable solutions that address the specific energy needs of underserved populations.

It is important to combine multiple approaches and leverage local knowledge and expertise to ensure effective and sustainable solutions for energy poverty and access gaps. Collaborative efforts among governments, organizations, communities, and technology providers are crucial for achieving universal energy access and addressing the associated socioeconomic challenges.

9.4 Policy recommendations for accelerating rural electrification: Accelerating rural electrification requires comprehensive policies that address various aspects of the electrification process. Here are some policy recommendations to accelerate rural electrification:

National Electrification Strategy: Develop a national electrification strategy that prioritizes rural electrification as a key goal. The strategy should outline targets, timelines, and key performance indicators to track progress. It should also identify funding sources and mechanisms to support electrification initiatives.

Enabling Policy and Regulatory Environment: Establish an enabling policy and regulatory environment that supports rural electrification. This includes streamlined processes for project approvals, licensing, and permits. Encourage policies that promote renewable energy deployment, decentralized systems, and innovative financing mechanisms. Ensure consistency and stability in policies to attract investment and facilitate long-term planning.

Financial Incentives and Subsidies: Provide financial incentives and subsidies to promote rural electrification. This can include tax incentives, grants, and subsidies for renewable energy projects and electrification infrastructure. Explore innovative financing mechanisms such as blended finance models, public-private partnerships, and results-based financing to attract investment and reduce financial barriers.

Targeted Funding Mechanisms: Establish dedicated funds or financing mechanisms to support rural electrification projects. These funds can be sourced from national budgets, international development assistance, or climate finance mechanisms. Prioritize funding for projects in remote and underserved areas to ensure equitable access to electricity.

Public-Private Partnerships: Encourage public-private partnerships (PPPs) to leverage private sector expertise, resources, and efficiencies in rural electrification. PPPs can bring in investment, technology, and management capabilities while ensuring public accountability and social inclusion. Develop standardized models for PPPs and create a conducive environment for private sector participation.

Capacity Building and Training: Implement capacity building programs to enhance technical and managerial skills in rural electrification. This includes training programs for local technicians, entrepreneurs, and community members in system installation, operation, and maintenance. Build institutional capacity within government agencies, utilities, and local organizations to effectively plan, implement, and manage electrification projects.

Community Engagement and Participation: Foster community engagement and participation in the electrification process. Involve local communities in project planning, implementation, and decision-making. Develop models of community ownership and management, such as cooperatives, to ensure long-term sustainability and community benefits. Empower communities with information, knowledge, and skills to actively participate in the electrification process.

Data Collection and Monitoring: Establish a robust data collection and monitoring system to track progress, measure impact, and inform decision-making. Collect data on energy access, demand patterns, and socio-economic indicators to identify areas of need and evaluate the effectiveness of electrification projects. Regular monitoring and evaluation help identify challenges, make informed policy decisions, and improve project implementation.

Integrated Approach to Development: Adopt an integrated approach to rural electrification that considers the linkages between energy access and other development sectors such as education, healthcare, agriculture, and entrepreneurship. Coordinate with relevant ministries and stakeholders to align electrification efforts with broader development goals and ensure a holistic approach to rural development.

Knowledge Sharing and Collaboration: Foster knowledge sharing and collaboration among stakeholders involved in rural electrification. Establish platforms for information exchange, best practice sharing, and lesson learning. Facilitate collaboration between government agencies, development organizations, research institutions, and private sector entities to leverage expertise, share experiences, and promote innovation in rural electrification.

By implementing these policy recommendations, governments can create an enabling environment, mobilize resources, and foster collaboration to accelerate rural electrification and bring sustainable electricity access to rural communities.

CHAPTER 10

CONCLUSION

10.1 Call to action for sustainable rural electrification: Call to Action:

Access to electricity is a fundamental necessity for the well-being and economic development of rural communities around the world. However, millions of people still lack access to reliable and affordable electricity, impeding their potential for growth and prosperity. To address this issue, we must rally together and take action towards sustainable rural electrification. Here's a call to action:

Policy and Investment: Governments, international organizations, and private investors should prioritize sustainable rural electrification in their policies and investment strategies. This includes allocating funds for electrification projects, creating supportive regulatory frameworks, and implementing incentives to attract private sector participation.

Renewable Energy Deployment: Embrace the power of renewable energy sources, such as solar, wind, hydro, and biomass, for rural electrification. Promote the development and deployment of off-grid and mini-grid solutions powered by renewables, tailored to the specific needs of rural communities. Prioritize decentralized energy generation to reduce transmission losses and increase energy access.

Technology Innovation: Foster innovation in energy technologies to drive down costs and improve the efficiency of rural electrification solutions. Encourage research and development of innovative energy storage systems, efficient appliances, and productive uses of electricity for income-generating activities in rural areas.

Capacity Building: Invest in training programs and capacity building initiatives to empower local communities, technicians, and entrepreneurs in rural areas. Provide education and vocational training on renewable energy technologies, maintenance, and management of electrification systems. This empowers communities to take ownership of their energy systems and ensures long-term sustainability.

Public-Private Partnerships: Foster collaborations between the public and private sectors to leverage expertise, resources, and funding. Public-private partnerships can accelerate the deployment of sustainable electrification solutions, create business opportunities, and ensure the provision of reliable and affordable electricity to rural communities.

Community Engagement: Involve local communities in the planning, implementation, and maintenance of rural electrification projects. Promote participatory approaches, conduct needs assessments, and incorporate community preferences and priorities. This ensures that electrification solutions are tailored to the specific needs and aspirations of rural communities.

Knowledge Sharing and Collaboration: Foster knowledge sharing and collaboration among stakeholders, including governments, organizations, academia, and local communities. Share best practices, lessons learned, and success stories to accelerate the adoption of sustainable rural electrification approaches. Collaborate on research, pilot projects, and policy development to create a collective impact.

Sustainable Development Integration: Recognize the interconnections between electrification and other aspects of sustainable development, such as education, healthcare, agriculture, and entrepreneurship. Integrate electrification efforts with initiatives in these sectors to maximize the socio-economic benefits and improve overall well-being in rural communities.

By responding to this call to action, we can make a significant difference in the lives of millions of people living in rural areas. Together, let's prioritize sustainable rural electrification, unlock the potential of communities, and work towards a more equitable and sustainable future for all.

10.2 Encouragement for further research and

collaboration: Further research and collaboration are essential for driving innovation, addressing global challenges, and unlocking new possibilities. Here is some encouragement to inspire and promote further research and collaboration:

Impactful Discoveries: Every significant breakthrough and innovation starts with research. By pursuing further research, you have the opportunity to make impactful discoveries that can shape the future, improve lives, and contribute to the advancement of knowledge in your field.

Solving Complex Problems: Many of the world's most pressing challenges, such as climate change, healthcare disparities, and poverty, require collaborative efforts and interdisciplinary research. By engaging in collaborative research, you can bring together diverse perspectives, expertise, and resources to tackle complex problems holistically.

Knowledge Expansion: Research is the foundation for expanding our understanding of the world. By conducting further research, you can delve deeper into existing knowledge, uncover new insights, and contribute to the growing body of knowledge in your field. This not only benefits your own understanding but also helps to build a solid foundation for future researchers.

Innovation and Technological Advancements: Collaboration plays a vital role in driving innovation and technological advancements. By collaborating with researchers, industry professionals, and other stakeholders, you can combine expertise and resources to develop groundbreaking technologies, solutions, and applications that have the potential to transform industries and improve quality of life.

Addressing Societal Challenges: Research and collaboration have the power to address societal challenges and create positive social impact. By focusing your efforts on pressing issues, such as poverty, inequality, and environmental sustainability, you can contribute to finding sustainable solutions and making a difference in the lives of people around the world.

Networking and Building Relationships: Engaging in collaborative research allows you to network and build relationships with fellow researchers, experts, and professionals in your field. These connections can lead to valuable collaborations, knowledge exchange, mentorship opportunities, and future partnerships, opening doors to new avenues of research and career development.

Funding and Support: Many research projects and collaborative endeavors receive funding and support from various sources, including government agencies, foundations, and industry partners. By actively pursuing research and collaboration, you increase your chances of accessing funding opportunities that can fuel your research and provide the necessary resources to bring your ideas to fruition.

Personal and Professional Growth: Engaging in further research and collaboration not only contributes to the advancement of knowledge but also facilitates personal and professional growth. It allows you to expand your skill set, develop critical thinking abilities, enhance your communication and teamwork skills, and gain a deeper understanding of your field of study.

Sharing and Disseminating Knowledge: Research is most impactful when its findings are shared and disseminated. By actively participating in research and collaboration, you have the opportunity to present your work at conferences, publish in academic journals, and engage in knowledge-sharing platforms. This enables you to contribute to the collective knowledge and inspire others in your field.

Leaving a Lasting Legacy: Research has the power to leave a lasting legacy. By pursuing further research and collaboration, you have the potential to make enduring contributions to your field, inspire future generations of researchers, and leave a positive impact on society for years to come.

Remember, research and collaboration are not solitary endeavors. By reaching out to fellow researchers, joining research groups, attending conferences, and actively seeking opportunities for collaboration, you can create a supportive network that amplifies your research impact and fosters a culture of innovation and progress.

REFERENCES.

Agrawal, R. (2008). Electricity in Rural India: A Case Study of Uttar Pradesh.

Anil, K. R. (2007). Empowering Rural Electrification: A Roadmap for India.

Anil, K. S. (2018). Rural Electrification: Challenges and Opportunities for Electrifying the Last Mile.

Arora, D., & Nandita, M. (2012). Rural Electrification: Strategies for Distributed Generation.

Ashok, S. (2010). Rural Electrification: A Review of Strategies and Experiences.

Barnes, D. F. (2007). The Challenge of Rural Electrification: Strategies for Developing Countries.

Benjamin, K. S. (2018). Rural Electrification: Strategies for Democratic Empowerment.

Bhattacharya, S. C., & Sudhakar, M. (2021). Energy for Rural Development: Renewable Resources and Technologies.

Bishop, M. L. (2015). Power to the People: Electrification Projects and the Politics of Development in Jamaica.

Chikere, N., & Chinedum, C. O. (2019). Rural Electrification: A Case Study of Nigeria.

Debashis, B. (2013). Rural Electrification in India: Strategies and Challenges.

Doheny-Farina, S. (2001). The Grid and the Village: Losing Electricity, Finding Community, Surviving Disaster.

Govindasamy, A. (2017). Rural Electrification: Through

Chukwujekwu John Okafor and Oko Obasi

Decentralized Off-grid Systems.

Hebblethwaite, B. (2015). Power to the People: Energy and the Cuban Nuclear Program.

Jacobson, A., et al. (2004). Rural Electrification: A Review of Socio-economic Impacts in Developing Countries.

Jeremy, F. (2018). Rural Electrification in Africa: An Assessment of Renewable Energy Technologies.

Jiawei, Z., & Shijie, C. (2014). Rural Electrification: A Case Study of China.

Joern, H. (2022). Rural Electrification: Empowering Communities through Renewable Energy.

Jon, E. (2010). Electricity Access and Rural Electrification: Insights from Nicaragua.

Kander, A., et al. (2013). Power to the People: Energy in Europe over the Last Five Centuries.

Kavita, R. (2009). Rural Electrification: Strategies and Lessons from Southeast Asia.

Khandelwal, P. K. (2010). Empowering Rural India: Connecting Rural Communities to Electricity.

Kirsty, D. (2011). Rural Electrification: A Handbook for Project Managers.

Komal, S. (2016). Rural Electrification: Harnessing Solar Power for Sustainable Development.

C h u k w u j e k w u   J o h n   O k a f o r   a n d   O k o
O b a s i
Kumar, P. (2018). Rural Electrification: Strategies and Implementation Challenges.

Maryanne, W. (2018). Solar-Powered Electricity for Developing Countries: A Practical Guide.

Md, Moinul I. (2017). Rural Electrification: A Case Study of Bangladesh.

Mohapatra, S. K., & Panda, S. K. (2020). Renewable Energy for Rural Electrification: Approaches and Case Studies from Developing Countries.

Nigel, S. (2019). Rural Electrification in the Developing World.

Padam, K. A. (2009). Rural Electrification: Strategies for Distributed Generation.

Padam, S., & Bhatnagar, S. S. (2008). Rural Electrification: Strategies and Practices.

Park, J.-B., & Lee, S.-H. (2012). Rural Electrification: Strategies for Distributed Generation.

Peter S. F. Y. (2017). Rural Electrification: Microgrids and Distributed Generation.

Pradeep, K. (2020). Rural Electrification: Policies and Practices for Sustainable Energy.

Rajanayagam, D. (2012). Rural Electrification: Technology Options, Planning, and Implementation.

Ramchandra, B. (2017). Rural Electrification: Strategies and Challenges in Developing Countries.

Ranjan, B. (2012). Rural Electrification: Through Decentralised Off-grid Systems in Developing Countries.

Richard, E. B. (2015). Rural Electrification: A Review of Policies and Programs.

Samir, K. K. (2012). Rural Electrification: Sustainable Development and Renewable Energy Approaches.

Skaggs, J. M. (1980). Electricity for Rural America: The Fight for the REA.

Sood, R. K. (2014). Rural Electrification: A Global Perspective.

Stephan, B. (2019). Rural Electrification: Lessons from Central and Eastern Europe.

Steven, H. C. (2005). The Electrification of Rural America.

Sudipta, B. (2000). Rural Electrification: Strategies for Distributed Generation.

Susmita, D. (2016). The Role of Renewable Energy in Rural Electrification: A Review and Case Study of Rural Electrification in India.

Thygesen, A. (2016). Rural Electrification: A Handbook for Development Workers and Engineers.

William, G. B., & Jha, R. K. (2011). Rural Electrification: Decentralised off-grid systems.

AUTHORS' PROFILE:

1.Engr. Chukwujekwu John Okafor:

Engr. Chukwujekwu John Okafor is a highly skilled and accomplished Electrical Engineer who hails from Awka, Anambra state, Nigeria. Engr. Chukwujekwu John Okafor has a strong passion for Electrical Engineering designs and installation.

As a registered Electrical Engineer with the Council for Regulation of Engineering in Nigeria (COREN), Engineer Okafor brings a wealth of expertise and experience to the development and implementation of electrification projects. He is a member, Anambra State Technical and Expatriate Monitoring Committee of Council for the Regulation Of Engineering in Nigeria.

Engr. Okafor's academic journey began at Nnamdi Azikiwe University, Awka, where he pursued his undergraduate studies in Electrical/Electronic Engineering. He further pursued a Master's degree in Engineering in Electronic/Telecommunication Engineering from the University of Benin.

Chukwujekwu John Okafor and Oko
Obasi

As one of the authors of the book "Empowering Communities: A Comprehensive Guide to Rural Electrification," Engr. Chukwujekwu John Okafor shares his vast knowledge, experiences, and insights gained over the course of his career. Through this comprehensive guide, he aims to inspire and equip fellow Engineers, policymakers, and development practitioners with the tools and understanding needed to embark on successful rural electrification projects.

2. Oko Obasi

Oko Obasi is a professional Life Coach based in Abuja,Nigeria. He has over twenty years experience that cuts across public and private sectors in Public Health consulting, Agriculture, E-commerce, Finance services & financial technology (fintech),legistative matters.

Having worked at the National Assembly as a Senior Legislative Aide and sits on the Board of several Non Governmental Organization such as Women in Africa for Aids Initiative(WINAA),Otabor Foundation For Medical Excellence and Leadership(OFLAME). He is the Founder and the first president of the global youth organization International Youth Development Forum(IYDF) which he founded in Braga, Portugal in 1996.

Chukwujekwu John Okafor and Oko Obasi

The Books written By Oko Obasi includes:Marriage Reloaded: From Eden to Zion,Goshen Exclusion,Effective Communication in Hospital Environment, Pinocchio Syndrome,Take Action: Shoot from plans to execution,and the latest best seller Sleep like a Baby, Wake like Royalty. He is married with children.

Chukwujekwu John Okafor and Oko Obasi